lack Students
White Schools

Edgar A. Epps, Editor

Black Students
in White Schools

THE NATIONAL SOCIETY
FOR THE STUDY OF EDUCATION

Series on Contemporary Educational Issues
Kenneth J. Rehage, Series Editor

The 1971 Titles

Accountability in Education, Leon M. Lessinger and Ralph W. Tyler, Editors
Farewell to Schools??? Daniel U. Levine and Robert J. Havighurst, Editors
Models for Integrated Education, Daniel U. Levine, Editor
PYGMALION Reconsidered, Janet D. Elashoff and Richard E. Snow
Reactions to Silberman's CRISIS IN THE CLASSROOM, A. Harry Passow, Editor

The 1972 Titles

Black Students in White Schools, Edgar A. Epps, Editor
Flexibility in School Programs, Willard J. Congreve and George J. Rinehart, Editors
Performance Contracting—1969-1971, James A. Mecklenburger
The Potential of Educational Futures, Michael Marien and Warren L. Ziegler, Editors
Sex Differences and Discrimination in Education, Scarvia Anderson, Editor

The National Society for the Study of Education also publishes Yearbooks which are distributed by the University of Chicago Press.

Inquiries regarding membership in the Society may be addressed to Kenneth J. Rehage, Secretary-Treasurer, 5835 Kimbark Avenue, Chicago 60637.

Black Students
in White Schools

edited by

Edgar G. Epps
The University of Chicago

Charles A. Jones Publishing Company
Worthington, Ohio

2   3   4   5   6   7   8   9   10   /   76   75   74   73

Library of Congress Catalog Card Number: 72-85889
International Standard Book Number: 0-8396-0024-0

Printed in the United States of America

Series Foreword

Black Students in White Schools is one of a group of five publications constituting the second set in a series prepared under the auspices of the National Society for the Study of Education. Other titles in this second set of paperbacks dealing with "Contemporary Educational Issues" are:

Performance Contracting—1969-1971, by James Mecklenburger

Sex Differences and Discrimination in Education, edited by Scarvia B. Anderson

Flexibility in School Programs, edited by Willard J. Congreve and George J. Rinehart

The Potential of Educational Futures, edited by Michael Marien and Warren L. Ziegler

The response to the first set of five paperbacks in this series, published in 1971, has been very encouraging. Like their predecessors the current volumes, all dealing with timely and significant issues in education, present a useful background and analysis for those who seek a deeper understanding of some of the critical educational problems of our times.

In this volume Professor Edgar G. Epps has brought together several original essays and has included two papers previously published elsewhere. While the various contributors focus on the problems of black students in white colleges, this book is by no means of interest only to persons concerned with higher education. It will deserve most thoughtful attention from educators at every level, for the problems with which it deals pervade the total educational scene. Each of the contributors addresses the theme of his essay from a vantage point enriched by personal experience.

The Society deeply appreciates the work done by Professor Epps as editor of this volume and by the various authors whose works have been included in this collection of illuminating essays on a very sensitive problem.

Kenneth J. Rehage
for the Committee on the Expanded Publication
Program of the National Society for the Study of Education

Contributors

Gordon D. Morgan, professor of sociology, The University of Arkansas, Fayetteville, Arkansas

Alexander W. Astin, director, Office of Research, American Council on Education

James M. Hedegard, visiting fellow, Institute for Research in Human Abilities, Memorial University, St. John's New Foundland, Canada

Edward J. Barnes, associate dean, College of Arts and Sciences, and director, University Community Educational Programs, University of Pittsburgh

William J. Wilson, associate professor of sociology, The University of Chicago

Lamar P. Miller, associate professor of educational administration, and education director of the Institute for Afro-American Affairs, New York University

Edgar G. Epps, Marshall Field IV Professor of Urban Education, The University of Chicago

Preface

This volume is concerned with the impact of a new student population on traditionally white colleges and universities and the reactions of the students to the intellectual and social climates in which they are expected to pursue their academic and social goals. The enrollment of relatively large numbers of students who do not share many of the traditional goals of institutions of higher learning raises serious questions about the function of higher education in American society. The new population includes many students who differ from the majority in socioeconomic background, career plans, and behavior patterns. College environments have usually been arranged on the assumption that the bulk of the student body will be white and middle class. Black students constantly find themselves faced with a struggle for survival in a "world they never made."

While the problems of black students are shared to some extent by all students from low socioeconomic status backgrounds, and to a greater extent by all students who are members of identifiable racial minorities, this book focuses exclusively on black students and their encounter with what John Edgerton has called the "White Sea of Higher Education." This small volume could not give adequate treatment to the problems of all groups which find themselves at odds with the American system of higher education.

Two chapters are reprints of articles which have appeared in other publications; the others were all prepared especially for this volume. Two articles report the results of original research. The other chapters are more properly viewed as "informed essays" written by persons who are thoroughly familiar with the situation under study through their knowledge of research and opinion in this area, and through personal experience in working with black students on white campuses. The authors of the original essays were asked to respond to the following set of questions when preparing their contributions: How do colleges and universities react to this new student population? What changes in the institutions seem most likely to minimize conflict or develop the students' capacity to cope with the academic environment? What mechanisms or adaptations do students use to maximize their individual and group abilities to cope with the academic institution? To what extent do institutional characteristics which are not necessary to the educational process create problems for minority group (or lower class) students?

The research and opinions presented in the following pages raise more questions than they answer. The Carnegie Commission on Higher Education has estimated that American colleges and universities must provide higher education for 1,100,000 black Americans by the year 1980 and for about 2,000,000 black Americans by the year 2000. This will require these institutions to reevaluate many of their deeply established policies and practices. We hope this book will help students of higher education, faculty members, and administrators to ask the types of questions that will lead to educational policies designed to provide education that black Americans will find both useful and rewarding.

Edgar G. Epps

Contents

Chapter

I. Introduction: A Brief Overview of Ghetto Education—Elementary to College, *Gordon D. Morgan*   1

Demotion of Schools to Ghetto Status, 4
Disadvantaged College Students, 5
Identifying Minority Group Talent, 8
Black Writers on Inner City Education, 11

II. Racial Considerations in Admissions, *Alexander W. Astin*   15

How Valid Are Traditional Admissions Criteria? 16
    Predicting Academic Achievement, 16; Predicting
    Who Will Drop Out, 21; Effects of the College, 24
The "Atypical" Student in the Selective College, 27
Effects of Race on Performance, 29
Are Admission Practices "Racist"? 33
Maintaining "Academic Standards," 34
Educating Students or Picking Winners? 35
Race as a Criterion in Admissions, 37
Institutional Responsibility for Specially-Admitted
    Students, 39
Conclusions, 39

III. Experiences of Black College Students at Predominantly White Institutions, *James M. Hedegard*   43

The Freshman Experience, 45
The Overall College Experience, 47
Some Special Nuances: Questions, Hypotheses, but
    Little Data, 55

Black Students at Black Colleges, 55; The Visibility of the Specially-Admitted Black Student, 55; The Critical Mass, 56; The Black Graduate Students, 56; Awareness "Of My Blackness," 57
Recommendations for Colleges and Universities, 57

IV. The Black Community and Black Students in White Colleges and Universities, *Edward J. Barnes*   60

Introduction, 60
The Black Community—Nature and Structure, 62
The Black College Student—Past and Present, 63
Emergence of Black Consciousness—Some Areas of Conflict, 65
Conflict with Environment, 70

V. The Quest for Meaningful Black Experience on White Campuses, *William J. Wilson*   74

VI. An Analysis of Objectives of Institutes and Departments of Afro-American Affairs, *Lamar P. Miller*   84

Ideological and Philosophical Perspectives, 86
An Overview of Present Practice, 89
Major Problems for Institutes, Departments, and Centers, 94
Realistic Objectives for the Future, 98

VII. Higher Education and Black Americans: Implications for the Future, *Edgar G. Epps*   102

College Attendance Rates, 102
Graduation, 103
The Role of Black Colleges, 104
Characteristics of Black Students in Biracial Colleges, 107
Recommendations, 110

I

Introduction:

A Brief Overview
of Ghetto Education—
Elementary to College

Gordon D. Morgan

The problem of inner city education has been building up since the abolition of slavery in the North. Escaped blacks often had no choice but to go to the low rent, less desirable sections of the cities where they tried to seek employment, however menial, and take advantage of whatever opportunities they found available. Public schooling was largely out of the question for them. Like whites, many blacks were discouraged from going to the non-private schools of the East and North because these schools were associated with institutions for paupers. Private schools operated by Quakers and other anti-slavery groups gave a few blacks who had an interest in formal training opportunities to acquire some education.

The first school operated regularly for blacks seems to have been started in New York City by Elias Neau, an Anglican, in 1704.(1)   By 1787, the Society of Friends and a black man, Thomas Sidney, of Philadelphia, started a school there.(2)   By 1822, there were no less than 22 schools for black children in Philadelphia.(3)   It is clear that the notion of separate education for black children prevailed in the North long before the Civil War.

As blacks became determined to obtain higher education, hesitant steps were taken to establish colleges for them. Avery College was started in Pittsburgh in 1852 and operated successfully until after the Civil War. In 1854, Ashmun Institute, which became Lincoln University in 1863, was established in Pennsylvania under

Presbyterian sponsorship. Wilberforce University, in Xenia, Ohio, was opened in 1855 by the Cincinnati Conference of the Methodist Episcopal Church. (4)

After the Civil War, the Freedmen's Bureau cooperated closely with Northern philanthropic and religious organizations in the establishment of such institutions as Howard University, Hampton Institute, St. Augustine's College, Atlanta University, and Fisk University. (5) The Morrill Act of 1890 (not to be confused with the Morrill Act of 1862 which established the basis for white land-grant institutions) made possible the establishment of separate Negro land-grant colleges in the southern and border states. Through this combination of philanthropy and government supported "separate-but-equal" institutions, more than 100 colleges and universities "for Negroes" were established. These colleges and universities produced nearly all of the college educated blacks in the United States before World War II and many of the college educated African leaders.

The migration of large numbers of blacks to Northern cities early in the twentieth century laid the foundation for current problems of ghetto education. There was some concern with ghetto education as early as the 1930's when such committees as those for better schools in Harlem were functioning. After the Harlem riots of 1935, Mayor Fiorello LaGuardia asked the sociologist, E. Franklin Frazier, to study the state of things in Harlem. Frazier then noted grave and flagrant deficiencies and injustices in the ghetto schools. (6)

In 1939, Professor Doxey A. Wilkerson was asked by the President's Advisory Committee on Education to do a study on Negro education. The Washington, D. C., ghetto engaged a principal part of his interest in that study. Wilkerson evidently thought that the segregated schools of the District were models which might be followed if separate schools for the races were to be maintained. He stated:

The public schools of the District of Columbia are illustrative of the policies and practices which might well be emulated by other communities with segregated schools. (7)

The District schools were so superior to the black schools of the South and most of the North that Wilkerson failed to consider the students themselves and the sociological forces at work which would soon define Washington, D. C., as one of the worst ghettos in the nation. (8)

Ghetto education was largely overlooked from the early 1940's through the early 1960's. In 1961 James B. Conant reported that in a slum area of 125,000 citizens, mostly black, 70 percent of girls and boys between the ages of 16 and 21 were out of school, unemployed, impoverished and discriminated against. They could become persons without attachments to their homes, communities or jobs. Big city schools were admonished to try harder to prepare these slum youths for meaningful employment. Conant suggested that schools expand their staffs, coordinate their efforts with employers, labor unions, youth welfare, and employment agencies. (9) Although conditions were disturbing in the ghetto schools generally, in some of the *worst* areas of New York City, Chicago, Detroit, and St. Louis, where blackboard jungles were expected, Conant found schools with high morale, tight discipline, and imaginative teachers and principals. (10)

Kenneth B. Clark's comprehensive study of the Harlem ghetto in the early 1960's was entitled, "Youth in the Ghetto: A Study of the Consequences of Powerlessness and a Blueprint for Change." This report detailed many depressing facts about ghetto life. It made such an impression on professional observers that Dr. Clark was encouraged to rework this report and present it in such a manner that a broadly based general readership could profit from it. His influential *Dark Ghetto* was the result, and his statement on the separate and unequal status of ghetto schools has, in the short time since its publication, become almost classic. Once more the hard problems of teaching and learning in inner city schools were stressed as well as analyses of the causes of these problems. (11)

Frank Riessman's *The Culturally Deprived Child* appeared in 1962.(12) It was immediately influential in its impact upon the teachers and educators interested in ghetto education. The theory of cultural deprivation was endorsed almost unequivocally at first, and in its wake were spawned a large number of books and articles using this concept as a theme. Scholars like Dr. Kenneth B. Clark reacted almost instantaneously to the *deprivation argument,* pointing out that it was based on the false logic that ghetto culture was inimical to school success. (13) Another important work, Patricia Sexton's *Education and Income,* showed that richer and more racially homogeneous schools had better facilities, better qualified staffs and therefore (?) higher scholastic achievement among the student bodies. (14)

Since about 1963 there have been a number of personal accounts of the difficulties of teaching in ghetto schools, particularly at the elementary and junior high levels. James Herndon's *The Way It Spozed To Be,* Robert Kendall's *White Teacher in a Black School,* Herbert Kohl's *36 Children,* Elizabeth Eddy's *Walk The White Line,* Jonathan Kozol's *Death at an Early Age,* and Nat Hentoff's *Our Children Are Dying* all fall into this category. The graphic pictures of the frustrations, challenges and rewards of ghetto teaching presented in these works are valuable accounts of the strategies which process children for failure in ghetto schools.

Disadvantaged elementary and junior high school children have received wide attention in the published literature, and libraries now have substantial numbers of books of readings on how to teach them. Joe L. Frost and Glenn R. Hawkes have edited a volume entitled the

Disadvantaged Child which is an example of the kind of work available. Another is Harry Passow's *Education in Depressed Areas.*

Demotion of Schools to Ghetto Status

Many educators have apparently forgotten, or did not know, that what are today routinely referred to as black slum schools were not always so viewed. The label of slum has been attached in most cases within the past fifteen years or near to the time of the decision in the 1954 *Brown* vs. *Board of Education of Topeka* case. Prior to then the big city black schools generally had viable programs, the most highly qualified and best paid teachers, better facilities and higher ratings than they are now accorded. Manassas High of Memphis, Froebel of Gary, DuSable of Chicago, Lincoln and Sumner of the Greater Kansas City area, Douglass of Oklahoma City, Parker of Birmingham, Jones and Dunbar of Greater Little Rock, and many others in cities of the North and South produced hundreds of leaders of contemporary black society. Teachers and students in the community were mutually and emotionally involved in community development. Extra effort was expended to make all proud of the school. The school was inseparable from the community and they proceeded together.

Writers on the problem of slum education often take the very immediate present as a point of departure for their analysis and do not go far into the historical development of the problems they observe. They do not seem to recognize the forces at work which have demoted the big city schools for blacks to slum status. Martin Trow, for example, does not seem to realize that perhaps no more than fifteen years ago he would have been in serious error in saying the big city black high schools were places where nobody wanted to teach.(15)   Just the opposite would have been true, at least for many black teachers. A job in a well-financed, large black city school was more attractive than a teaching post in a small, rural, or small town school, white or black in the South or Midwest. It became expedient to define the slum school as a problem only when it developed that black children would be in the majority in schools attended by whites. While these schools catered totally to a black clientele, they tended to be held up as models which black schools were encouraged to emulate and their slum qualities were not emphasized.

The deterioration of slum schools and the attendant miseducation of black children has now become a serious problem for the major colleges and universities. For most of the past century, the burden of providing higher education for black youths who had been poorly educated in inferior elementary and secondary schools fell upon the poorly financed and undermanned black colleges. Since 1965, however, pressures from civil rights organizations and the federal government have resulted in the admission of a relatively large number of ghetto students to white four-year colleges and universities. While their numbers are still small in proportion to the white student population (less than three percent at most colleges and universities), nevertheless these institutions have been hard pressed to to develop programs which would provide a meaningful education for this new student population.

Disadvantaged College Students

In Frost and Hawkes' extensive bibliography of research studies on poor students, one finds no mention of articles dealing with problems of teaching college students from disadvantaged circumstances and slums. (16)

Aside from scattered articles appearing in the *Journal of Negro Education,* inner city college students have hardly been studied. Even there, reports are more the result of informal observation than of systematic inquiry. How to teach students from ghetto backgrounds has been of less concern than keeping track of their numbers and noting their shortcomings in comparison with whites. Very few ghetto students, proportionately speaking, have been going to college. The *Riot Commission* reported that less than 1 percent of Harlem youth go to college. (17) In cities such as Minneapolis-St. Paul, ghetto blacks have been too few on the local campuses to merit attention as a category. Before passage of the Higher Education Act of 1965 when student loans and work study programs enabled many poor students to enroll in college, not much attention was paid to inner city students. Some qualified for help under the earlier National Defense Education Act loan program, but perhaps the real impetus came after 1965. John Egerton's data, which is most recent, shows that in schools in states where the big ghettos are found, no more than 2 percent of the student bodies are black. (18)

Irene R. Kiernan and Roy P. Daniels studied 23 Negro students in a community college in a large Eastern city. All of these students were from poor families. None of their family members had been to college or had held skilled jobs. Alcoholism, desertion, illegitimacy, transiency, and near financial destitution would be more descriptive of the conditions from which they came. Of interest is their almost categorical "what's the use?" attitude in relation to studying hard and obtaining future rewards of a "good" job. The researchers concluded that these students were trying to make the transition from lower-class to middle-class status and in the process became anxiety ridden, bitter, and cynical toward themselves and the groups into which they desired entrance. (19)

N. J. Johnson, N. Gilbert, and R. Wyer found, after controlling for a number of variables such as percent of black students in a high school, that based on the grades of 121 black and 250 white freshmen at the University of Illinois (Chicago Circle Campus), social class orientation and lack of interracial conflict facilitated learning experiences. (20) Their findings are particularly relevant in view of the fact that students from a predominantly black high school with a "middle-class orientation" received better grades than did black students who attended a biracial school with a "lower-class orientation." The lower-class orientation variable seems to be a more potent predictor of success in the middle-class world of the white university than the race variable. These results are based on a small sample in one university, but they are suggestive in their implications.

In 1961, Jacqueline P. Wiseman found that motivation and academic achievement were highly related. Level of achievement was found to vary with degree of integration into college life. Low participation in extra-curricular activities and lack of interest in increasing school spirit were closely related to lower academic achievement. (21) Although her study was not with ghetto students, her message is clear. Studies and personal observations consistently reveal that most black students on large white campuses are not highly involved in campus activities. The current emphasis on *blackness* has opened avenues whereby black organizations could be created and it is around the activities of these organizations that black student activities center. (22)

Leslie Berger suggests that environment and educational systems conspire to rob students of motivation and deny poor students realistic chances to acquire skills taken for granted in middle-class children. He argues against assuming, in the case of ghetto youths, that past performance is a direct function of ability. He notes that these students show evidence of distrust of the establishment, defeatism, and hostility. As with some elementary teachers, some college teachers do not believe their students are educable. Teacher patience is short. They react with hostility when tested by students. Still other teachers are over-protective and concerned with whether or not ghetto students like them. Some inner city students who cannot keep up academically camouflage their needs and rely on group unity to prove to the establishment that it is not considering their needs. (23)

E. Gordon and D. Wilkerson have produced a most useful compendium of data and commentary on education of ghetto students, though they use the term *compensatory* to describe needs and practices relating to them. They found that compensatory programs were, for the most part, with white students. Programs were more frequent among institutions like liberal arts junior colleges or Ph.D. granting institutions. Half of the 610 institutions surveyed were working with no more than 30 students who were considered as disadvantaged. A more recent survey by Gordon and his colleagues (in process) indicates that by 1969, the majority of schools reporting still operated programs assisting 50 or fewer students. The majority of these programs have as their aim the bringing of students from hostile, different, or indifferent backgrounds up to a level where they can be reached by existing educational practices. (24)

Prior to the burning of Watts, studies of inner city education seemed to focus on the students, teachers, and facilities in sub-collegiate schools. It had not generally been considered of much importance that many ghetto youths were somehow making it to college. As early as the 1930's it had been the custom for southern black colleges to recruit football players, musicians, and other students with special talents from the ghettos of the North, where high schools were larger, having better programs and where the range of talent was wide. Even then faculty members at black colleges noted behaviors of the big city students which set them apart from the masses of Southern black students. Conflict often arose between southern rural and northern urban students. The latter group considered the former backward, and the former considered the latter as "cocky" and exhibiting a bearing of superiority. Big city students were disproportionately involved in disciplinary problems owing to their more frequent deviations from school rules. (25)

After Watts, northern schools near the slums started to show interest in ghetto students. Part of their motivation has been based on the fear that ghetto violence might spread from the streets to their campuses and their buildings might be burned down. Federal money awarded to many colleges for their "disadvantaged programs" has encouraged them to do something about the youths from the slums who end up in college. Some colleges have dared to go out, in a burst of zeal, and recruit black slum students. These programs have helped few slum youths because they have been too limited in the groups they reach, they rarely go for the hard core black youth. (26) In fact, colleges have placed in special programs many youths from the ghetto who had no problems other than poverty. The label of "disadvantaged" has been used to justify doing a little for the blacks in order to qualify for the "federal dollar," without a serious commitment by the majority of colleges and universities involved to helping these students and changing ineffective and discriminatory social structures.

Basically, there has been little change of attitude regarding the educability of the ghetto blacks by the institutions of higher learning. Even when Arthur Jensen, (27) the latest of the white authorities to argue black genetic inferiority, takes his negative position, white scholars generally do not make him suffer through the pangs of condemnation for drawing faulty conclusions from faulty premises and biased data. Unless blacks condemn the Jensens, their words are spread as gospel truths. (It is recognized that some whites have condemned the Jensens, but not enough to make any real impact on the thinking of the white masses.)

The prevailing attitude of white institutions is that black students are social problems rather than students with problems; that they make such small contributions to school and academic life that if federal funds were not forthcoming to subsidize their presence, blacks would be left, as in the past, to fester and frustrate in the ghetto.

It is clear that it is not inconsistent with white expectations to have persistent black ignorance, poverty, disease, and hardship and this is why structural changes are not readily made to enable blacks to help themselves. College is still many times an experience which the establishment whites do not wish to see blacks engage in routinely. The production of too many educated blacks has serious implications for the power structures attuned to the need for a cheap labor supply and who realize that given equal competitive opportunities many whites will not be successful in the struggle. Hence, whites with this orientation try to make college as irrelevant as possible for blacks or to so twist them up psychologically that they turn into "black revolutionaries" bound to lose in a physical encounter with the police forces of the nation. (28) The case of Angela Davis is a good example of the twisting effect college can have on the black student.(29)

Studies of black college youth, like studies of black people generally, have been centered for the most part around their pathologies. (30) The assumption is made that something is wrong with the student as a person, or with black culture, which militates against his learning. Writers like Robert Bell suggest that black militancy hinders black learning. Bell believes the black student militant is now the most revolutionary of all the students. The militant believes strongly that America is racist and sees some justification in sit-ins, property destruction and assaults on police.(31)   It does not require great sophistication to see or imagine the consequences defining a category of students as revolutionary. It leads to a conception of them as being unteachable, hostile, and merely to be tolerated on campus.

A basic problem confronting those who seek to educate youths from the ghetto is the lack of an institutional philosophy of education to serve as a guide. This is, of course, brought about by the fact that there is no firm commitment to the training of the ghetto youth by the educational establishment. (32) Each level of the educational ladder which the ghetto youth ascends ushers him into greater uncertainty as to what the outcome will be for him. He is, no doubt, more uncertain when he finishes a baccalaureate program about where he might function in the system than when he completed junior or senior high school when he accepted as given that he was not fully prepared for meaningful employment.

Identifying Minority Group Talent

For years it has been known that minority group youth are not choosing professions and fields which reflect their abilities, proper guidance, and community needs. In the former segregated colleges of the South, there were few faculty persons skilled and willing enough to help a youth reach a real assessment of his potential for performance in a particular field. Moreover, the social structure was so closed that, regardless of counseling, a black youth was limited largely to teaching and other segregated professions such as theology and medicine. He did not need counseling to go into traditional employment in the ghetto, cleaning and pressing, cosmetology, domestic work, undertaking, preaching, and cooking. Practically, the student's choice of a major reflected estimates of the need for teachers and other professionals within the segregated social structure. A student counseled into mathematics simply expected to be a mathematics teacher. One showing manual dexterity might be advised to study trades and to possibly expect to become a small, private, self-employed practitioner or perhaps a teacher of some shop or trade course in a public school.

First generation black college students were, and still are, badly counseled into fields. They have few earlier models to follow within their families. Moreover, school counselors do not understand much about how to advise the minority student who does not verbalize well. Test scores are the basis on which students are usually encouraged or discouraged from entering training for particular fields and professions. For minority students, without notions of what they might be able to do because of an absence of models and because of depressed scores, the choice of what to train for becomes haphazard. In most cases they continue toward those fields which are showing signs of becoming overcrowded, like elementary and secondary teaching.

These students have confidence that they can complete these curricula because they have seen many of their acquaintances do so. They have less confidence in their ability to complete non-traditional curricula even though such curricula may not involve more difficult subject matter or technical procedures.

There is a desperate need to identify minority group talent and to redistribute it so that students take advantage of a wider spectrum of college and university offerings to prepare them for a wider variety of fields. There is evidence that this cannot be done so long as counselors insist on using the traditional indices of student interest and abilities in fields. In fact, youths coming from the restricted conditions of the slums or small towns may not be aware of the tremendous range of positions to which they might realistically aspire. A youth can hardly show interest in a field of which he is virtually unaware. A counselor cannot be of much help to a student from outside the mainstream if traditional evidence of ability and interest is the determining criterion on which a decision is made. For example, it is recognized widely that slum and poor black youth are generally good athletes showing outstanding eye, hand, and muscular coordination. They may be deficient in verbal skills of the middle class variety reflecting their lack of exposure to or emphasis on formal academic or classroom learning. They may have the manual dexterity required to be dentists or optometrists or other highly technical mechanics but would be discouraged from training for these fields because of depressed scores on verbal facility and curricular biases which favor academic analytic skills.

College personnel who are in positions to influence the direction of training of minority youth are often unable to identify talent unless it is within their individual fields. Students who do not show the traditional signs of potential in the faculty person's field may simply be labeled as "unpromising," and left to stagnate. Such a student may be encouraged to go into a less prestigious, demanding, or promising field even if that field is impractical in terms of the needs of the type of community in which the minority person is very likely to work.

While it is known that many minority group youths suffer from academic deficits, too often these are treated as lack of ability to do different types of non-academic work. The two-year general education program of a typical college or university is where most of the encouragement or discouragement is given a youth to enter a particular field. A student may infer from his failure to master the range of academic mathematics (say, through the calculus) that he cannot do the arithmetic required to be a dentist, pharmacist, or mechanic though these fields may not require the level of mathematics he failed to master. The student may feel that because he flunks a course once or twice he simply cannot master that course. The chances are that he could easily master the practical mathematics or science required in a variety of fields in which he might develop an interest and eventually achieve competence. However, drastic changes in undergraduate and professional programs are needed before such students will be allowed to develop competence in such fields.

Within the minority group category there is grossly poor counseling by sex. Females, in particular, are not encouraged to pursue useful careers which are non-traditional for their sex though they are often far ahead of males academically. Almost without regard for ability, the minority female is pointed toward fields which may not be very useful but such women may be, by training, relatively more teachable, unproblematic socially and more meticulous in their work. They may be more easily financed through funds for poor students and less likely to let emotions associated with social and inter-personal problems interfere with their training. Ordinarily they do not have plans which would be complicated by further study, such as draft problems. Because the minority female has gone into traditional fields, regardless of her potential for achievement in other fields, she is continually pushed toward those fields though she may be equally promising in other work. In the 24-year integrated history of the University of Arkansas, for example, there has been only one black woman who enrolled in and completed the curriculum in law. Two have gained medical degrees. Black female scholars in the hard and soft sciences have been numerically sufficient (academically also) to generate a greater output than this this if systematic factors such as poor counseling were not at work.(33) The general society as well as the *de facto* segregated communities need the skills these young ladies could acquire, but traditional counseling and limited perspectives prohibit their movement toward the acquisition of skills and training more immediately useful.

Black Writers
on Inner City Education

Black writers on inner city education have been handicapped and unable to concentrate on the real problems of educating slum youth. Many, if not most, have been busy trying to refute the racist claims made by unsympathetic white writers. Because so much of the literature on black educational disadvantage centers on elementary and secondary students, most of the reactions of black scholars have focused on these levels. Arguments have been over such matters as the relationship between social class and school performance, teacher attitudes towards their schools and students, the I.Q. and grouping controversy, and the general consequences of cultural deprivation on learning. (34)

At the college level, black writers have been less active, partly because at that level the problems of social class, I.Q. and teacher attitudes are not most relevant. Student motivation is not much of a problem because students are paying their way, at least partially, and will be dropped when their grades fall below a certain norm even if they are receiving federal aid. The black students are on the campus and the issue is not whether they are intelligent enough or high enough in class status to profit from college experience. The basic question is what kind of experience will be most beneficial.

A considerable amount of black writing on the college student has concerned the technical question of admissions. Black students have agitated for admissions changes in the more prestigious schools mainly because they conceive of the requirements as irrelevant or racist. These students have exerted but little effort to force black colleges to alter their admissions criteria which, in most cases, were the same as those of their sister white institutions. Generally, however, the black schools required lower minimum entrance test scores. The difference,, of course, was that white schools wanted more money for attendance and could apply differential standards to poor whites and blacks when they wanted to keep their numbers small on their campuses. Research into the validity of admissions criteria such as grades and achievement tests has led black writers to question whether schools were aiming simply to screen out students, white or black, who were not wanted on campus. This tactic permitted the preservation of the campuses as islands of privilege and prestige for the affluent (mainly white). (35)   Robert Green states, after a careful review of admissions criteria:

If we are to make an impact on the . . . nation . . . along with educating the white community regarding its own racism, we must provide black and other minority students with an opportunity for higher education. If this is to be done, traditional admissions criteria (standardized aptitude tests and high school grades) must be carefully assessed. . . . But when (minority students are) admitted to college and given proper tutorial and counseling services (both personal and academic), their chances for success are greatly enhanced. . . . The foremost challenge to predominantly white institutions of higher learning is to evaluate carefully and reconsider those admission policies of many years' standing in order to provide all segments of our society with an opportunity to share in programs of higher education. (36)

Black writers have continued to point out the fundamentally and subtly racist nature of higher education and the impact of racist practices and policies on black collegians. (37)

Harry Edwards recently assessed the programs and ideologies of black students as they seek education on predominantly white campuses. His categories (radical activist, militant, revolutionary, anomic activist and conforming Negro) are useful. Their social origins and attitudes toward school work suggest the extent to which institutions must go to come to terms with these students. (38)

Edwards and others have not, in general, separated black youth according to the nature of their spatial socialization. Those raised in slums have been lumped with those blacks raised in other circumstances. Morgan tries to remedy this problem by differentiating between ghetto and other black students. (39) There were few slum college youth for many years as the colleges sought to exclude all who came from deviate cultural backgrounds. The marches by Dr. Martin Luther King, Jr., the numerous sit-ins, the ghetto rebellions beginning with Watts, Black Power, black awareness, the loss of magnetism of white culture and HEW regulations regarding student aid, all combined to force white colleges to admit more blacks, including those from the ghettos. Special programs have been mounted for these students, though ostensibly for all who needed them. A cadre of faculty and administrators with skills in handling ghetto youth is building up on some large campuses. The usual strategy, of course, is to hire blacks for one set of duties and then expect them to work closely with and control black students. Even new colleges have been started to cater to these students and their problems and today about twelve predominantly black colleges are found in cities with the largest and most problematic ghettos. (40)

The typical youth from the ghetto is found to exhibit a defeatist attitude relative to academic work. He must be dragged to success rather than given a gentle push which combines with his own initiative to keep him moving. He is insecure by virtue of having had no stable home life. His insecurity is often shown in terms of temper tantrums, manipulation of teachers, misplaced aggressiveness and inability to confront authority figures without resorting to infantile responses. He is a mass man showing his basic feelings in crowds rather than in individualistic ways. He is oriented toward beating the system in whatever form it is found. To him, illicit channels of operation are more intriguing than legitimate ones for achieving social mobility. He is very race conscious and is barely tolerant of white people for his own experience has been heavily conditioned by the realities of poor race relations. (41)

Notes

(1) H. M. Bond, *Education of the Negro in the American Social Order* (New York: Prentice-Hall, 1934), p. 369.

(2) *Ibid.,* p. 368.

(3) *Ibid.,* p. 370.

(4) John Hope Franklin, *From Slavery to Freedom* (New York: Vintage Books Edition, 1969), p. 231.

(5) *Ibid.,* p. 308.

(6) See in K. B. Clark, *Dark Ghetto* (New York: Harper and Row, 1965), p. 118.

(7) D. A. Wilkerson, "Special Problems of Negro Education," (Washington, D. C.: U. S. Government Printing Office, 1969) p. 155.

(8) Andrew Kopkind and James Ridgeway, "Washington: The Lost Colony," *The New Republic* (April 1966): 13-17.

(9) James B. Conant, *Slums and Suburbs* (New York: McGraw-Hill, 1961).

(10) James B. Conant, "Dynamite in our Large *Cities," Crime and Delinquency,* (April 1962): 103-112.

(11) Clark, *op. cit.*

(12) Frank Riessman, *The Culturally Deprived Child* (New York: Harper and Row, 1962).

(13) Clark, *op. cit.,* pp. 129-133.

(14) Patricia Sexton, *Education and Income* (New York: Viking, 1961).

(15) See Martin Trow, "Two Problems in American Public Education," in R. R. Bell and H. R. Stub, *The Sociology of Education* (Homewood, Illinois: The Dorsey Press, 1968), pp. 16-18.

(16) Joe L. Frost and Glenn R. Hawkes, *The Disadvantaged Child* (Boston: Houghton Mifflin Company, 1966).

(17) U. S. Riot Commission Report, otherwise known as the *Report of the National Advisory Commission on Civil Disorders* (New York: E. P. Dutton, 1968), p. 452.

(18) John Egerton, *State Universities and Black Americans* (Atlanta: Southern Reporting Service, 1969), pp. 17-19.

(19) Irene R. Kiernan and Roy P. Daniels, "Signs of Social Change Through an Exploratory Study of 23 Negro Students in a Community College" *Journal of Negro Education* (Spring 1967): 129-135.

(20) N. J. Johnson, N. Gilbert and R. Wyer, "Quality Education and Integration: An Exploratory Study," *Phylon* (Fall 1967): 221-229.

(21) Jacqueline P. Wiseman, "Achievement and Motivation in a College Environment," *Berkeley Journal of Sociology* (Spring 1961): 35-51.

(22) See "What Black College Students Want from You," *College Management,* (March 1969): 32-57. See also Charles Willie and Joan D. Levy, "Black is Lonely," *Psychology Today* (March, 1972): 50.

(23) Leslie Berger, "University Programs for Urban Black and Puerto Rican Youth," *The Record* (Fall 1968): 382-388.

(24) E. Gordon and D. Wilkerson, *Compensatory Education for the Disadvantaged* (New York: College Entrance Examination Board, 1966), p. 158. See especially their critique of compensatory education, pp. 156-189. Students often resent the special efforts undertaken in their behalf because there is a kind of stigma associated with being "special" and having a need for "compensatory" or "remedial" programs. See, for example, G. Louis Heath, "An Inquiry Into a University's 'Nobel Savage' program," *Integrated Education* (July-August, 1970): 4-9.

(25) Suggested by teachers and administrators with long time experience in black colleges.

(26) Thomas Sowell, argues that too often deserving students are ignored in favor of "hard core" ghetto students. *New York Times Magazine* (December 13, 1970): 36.

(27) Arthur R. Jensen, "How Much Can We Boost I.Q. and Scholastic Achievement?" *Harvard Educational Review* 39, 1 (1969): 1-123.

(28) L. M. Killian in *The Impossible Revolution? Black Power and the American Dream* (New York: Random House, 1968) pp. 147-176, argues this point quite thoroughly.

(29) Herbert Marcuse at Brandeis, the eclectic Marxist philosopher, was the most influential of the several instructors Angela studied with who helped her to espouse a revolutionary strategy at the wrong time in her career and in the life of the black movement. Angela became so system conscious she had difficulty in maintaining any sort of detachment from action, even as a matter of strategy. See "The Angela Davis Case," *Newsweek* (October 26, 1970): 18-24. There is probably a revolutionary tendency in a majority of black students emerging from the colleges of today, particularly the white ones.

(30) See for example, Edwin W. McClain, "Personality Characteristics of Negro College Students in the South—A Recent Appraisal," *Journal of Negro Education,* 36, 3 (1967): 320-325.

(31) Robert R. Bell, *Social Deviance* (Homewood, Illinois: Dorsey, 1971), p. 424.

(32) See, for example, Randall H. Harber, "Georgia: Black Recruitment Lags at University," *South Today,* 3, 2, (September 1971): 6-7.

(33) Sexism may be the basis of much of this poor counseling. One student reported that she and other women students in her pharmacy class were constantly reminded that they were occupying slots that should be held by males who would have families to support while the females would do nothing with their professional training. (Ed.)

(34) See, for example, Kenneth B. Clark, "Educational Stimulation of Racially Disadvantaged Children," in A. H. Passow, ed., *Education in Depressed Areas* (New York: Teachers College Press, 1963), pp. 142-161.

(35) Convincing evidence of the educability of students from peer backgrounds with low verbal facility scores is being mounted. See, W. M. Brown and R. D. Russell, "Limitations of Admissions Testing for the Disadvantaged," *Personnel and Guidance Journal,* 43 (November 1964): 301-304; *New York Times,* "Open Admissions at City University" (July 12, 1969): 9; *School and Society,* "Operation Seek," 94: 374 (November 12, 1966): 376; and D. Metzger Miller and P. O'Connor, "Achiever Personality and Academic Success Among Disadvantaged College Students," *Journal of Social Issues,* XXV, 3 (1969): 103-116.

(36) R. L. Green, "The Black Quest for Higher Education: An Admissions Dilemma," *Personnel and Guidance Journal,* 47, No. 9 (May 1969): p. 910. Copyright by American Personnel and Guidance Association.

(37) See at many places in William Moore, Jr., "Student Groups Assessing Their Colleges and Universities," in F. F. Harcleroad and J. H. Cornell, editors, *Assessment of Colleges and Universities* (Iowa City, Iowa: The American College Testing Program, 1971), pp. 23-25.

(38) See Harry Edwards, *Black Students* (New York: Free Press, 1970).

(39) G. D. Morgan, *The Ghetto College Student: A Descriptive Essay on College Youth From the Inner City* (Iowa City, Iowa: The American College Testing Program, 1970).

(40) See Preston Valien, "Some Perspectives on Advancing the Role of Blacks in Higher Education," address at the University of Arkansas, Summer, 1971, p. 5, mimeographed.

(41) Morgan, *op. cit.,* pp. 44-54.

II

Racial
Considerations
in Admissions

Alexander W. Astin

Controversy over race in higher education frequently centers on the admissions process. These conflicts, though focusing on black students or other student minority groups, raise certain more fundamental questions about the entire rationale of admissions as practiced in American colleges and universities. The purpose of this paper is to elucidate these basic questions in the context of racial considerations in college admissions.

Many people are concerned about the relatively low proportions of black students who are admitted to college and about the widespread *de facto* segregation that exists in our institutions. The basic facts about the racial composition of student bodies are now known. Among the 1.5 million new freshmen who entered college in 1968, between 6 and 7 percent were black. (1) Even though many colleges have gone to considerable effort recently to recruit more black students, our evidence indicates that the proportion of blacks among entering freshmen has changed only slightly since 1966. (2) In short, the representation of blacks among new college students is far below their representation in the college-age population (about 12 percent) and shows little evidence of increasing. Furthermore, those blacks who do attend college are not distributed evenly among the various types of institutions. Nearly half of the black freshmen, for example, attend predominantly Negro colleges, where the number of white students averages less than 3 percent. (3) Moreover, black students attending predominantly white colleges are concentrated in a relatively small number of instututions; more than *half* of all the institutions in the country enroll freshman classes in which blacks make up less than 2 percent. (4)

How Valid
Are Traditional
Admissions Criteria?

Traditionally, colleges have selected their applicants primarily on the basis of their secondary school grades and their scores on tests of academic aptitude. While other criteria—sex, geographic region, athletic ability, and so forth—are frequently taken into account, most institutions probably judge most applicants on the basis of evidence of academic merit. In the face of the expanding demand for higher education among secondary school youth, colleges have become highly sophisticated in applying these merit criteria, even to the point of eliminating large numbers of student applicants solely by means of computer analyses of test scores and grades.

There is little question that the average black high school student compares unfavorably with the average white on these merit criteria, particularly on tests of academic ability. Consequently, the blind application of such criteria in college admissions will result in (a) proportionately fewer blacks than whites being admitted and (b) partial segregation of the races, with few blacks being admitted to the most selective institutions.

The use of high school grades and aptitude test scores in college admissions is most often defended on the grounds that these measures predict subsequent achievement in college. And indeed they do, as recent reviews of the literature show. (5) A point that is frequently overlooked, however, is that these predictions are subject to a considerable amount of *error*; not all of the most promising students succeed in college, nor do all the least promising students fail.

Predicting Academic Achievement

Data from a recent nationwide study of academic achievement and survival in college (6) provide an opportunity to examine—in practical terms—the degree of error associated with predicting college achievement from high school grades and test scores. These data were obtained from 36,581 students (19,524 men and 17,057 women) who enrolled at 180 different colleges and universities in the fall of 1966. Table 1 shows the relationship between the students' grades in high school and their freshman college grades. Clearly, a student's college grades are usually consistent with his high school grades. For example, boys who had A averages in high school obtained freshman year grade-point averages (GPAs) that were more than one full letter grade above the freshman averages obtained by boys with high school C averages. A similar tendency is apparent among girls.

Another way of looking at the relationship between high school and college grades is to examine the student's chances of obtaining a particular college grade-point average. The college letter grade of B or better (GPA of 2.50 or higher) would seem to represent a moderate level of academic "success." The results are shown in the last two columns of Table 1. About three-fourths of the men who had A or A+

TABLE 1

Predicting Freshman College Grades
from High School Grades
(N = 19,524 men and 17,057 women)

Average Grade in High School	Number of Students		Freshman Year College Grades			
			Mean GPA		Percentage with GPA of 2.50 (*B* Grade) or Higher	
	Men	Women	Men	Women	Men	Women
A or A+............	1,262	1,686	2.94	3.08	76	84
A−................	2,035	2,732	2.67	2.83	61	73
B+................	3,324	3,893	2.41	2.59	44	56
B.................	4,247	4,174	2.18	2.34	29	37
B−................	3,121	1,982	2.07	2.15	22	24
C+................	3,094	1,644	1.92	2.02	15	15
C.................	2,312	927	1.77	1.83	10	10
D.................	129	19	1.61	1.73	9	16

averages in high school achieved at least a B average as college freshmen, whereas only 10 percent of the men who had C averages in high school did so. In other words, boys with an A average in high school were *seven times* more likely than were boys with a C average in high school to obtain a B average in college, and A average boys were more than *twice* as likely to obtain a B average in college as were boys with a B average in high school.

Though the relationship between high school grades and college grades is consistent, it is far from perfect. For example, one-fourth of the boys who had A averages in high school failed to make even a B average in college. Similarly, 10 percent of both the boys and the girls who obtained only C averages in high school managed to obtain a B average or better in their freshman college year. This substantial amount of error in prediction is reflected in the correlations of only .50 and .51 between high school and college grades for men and women, respectively.

How accurately do scores on tests of academic ability predict the student's college grades? To facilitate discussion, we divided our sample of students into eleven levels on the basis of their scores on tests taken in high school. These ability levels are shown in Table 2, together with the number of students at each level and the percentage who obtained freshman GPAs of B or better. There is, obviously, a positive relationship between how well a student performs on a test of

TABLE 2

Predicting Freshman College Grades from Aptitude Test Scores

Level of Scores on Academic Aptitude Tests	NMSQT Selection [a]	SAT V + M [b]	ACT Composite [c]	Number of Students	Percentage Obtaining an Average of *B* or Better
11.......	151 or higher	1470 or higher	32 or higher	323	74
10.......	143–150	1381–1469	30–31	1,200	67
9.......	135–142	1297–1380	29–30	2,437	63
8.......	127–134	1216–1296	28–29	3,328	56
7.......	119–126	1134–1215	26–27	4,730	50
6.......	111–118	1055–1133	24–25	5,079	40
5.......	103–110	980–1054	23–24	5,266	38
4.......	95–102	907– 979	21–22	4,522	31
3.......	87– 94	838– 906	19–20	3,515	25
2.......	79– 86	770– 837	17–18	2,413	21
1.......	78 or lower	769 or lower	16 or lower	3,768	16

[a] National Merit Scholarship Qualifying Test selection scores.
[b] Scholastic Aptitude Test, Verbal and Mathematics scores.
[c] American College Test composite scores.

academic ability administered during high school and his grades as a college freshman. A student at the highest level of academic aptitude [11], for example, had more than four times as much chance of obtaining a B average or better in college as did a student at the lowest level of academic ability [1]: 74 chances in 100 versus only 16 chances in 100. However, test scores are less closely related to college grades than high school grades are. For example, 74 percent of the students at the highest test score level obtained B averages or better, as compared to 76 percent of the men and 84 percent of the women at the highest grade level (see Table 1). Moreover, students at the top level with respect to test scores represented a highly select group (only 323), compared with those in the highest average grade category from Table 1 (1,262 men and 1,686 women). An examination of the lowest-level categories in Tables 1 and 2 reveals a similar discrepancy favoring high school grades over academic aptitude scores as predictors of college grades. Of the 3,768 students at the lowest level of academic ability as measured by test scores, for example, 16 percent obtained B averages or better in college. However, if all the students who obtained high school averages of C+ or lower (more than twice as many as are at the lowest aptitude level) are grouped together, the overall percentage obtaining B averages or better in college is only 13.

The closer relationship between high school grades and college grades is reflected in the correlation coefficients: the correlations of freshman GPA with aptitude test scores are .35 and .43, respectively, for men and women, as compared to the correlations of .50 and .51 between freshman GPA and high school grades.

High school grades, then, are clearly the better predictors of freshman GPA. But another question arises here: Is a knowledge of the student's scores on aptitude tests superfluous, or will our predictions of college GPA be more accurate if we use high school grades and aptitude test scores *in combination*? To explore this possibility, we sorted all 36,581 students into 88 cells (8 grade levels x 11 test scores levels). The percentage obtaining freshman GPAs of B or better, computed separately for the students in each cell, is shown in Table 3. Selecting any level of aptitude and reading across the row,

TABLE 3

Chances in 100 of Obtaining an Average Grade of B (or Better) during the First Year of College as a Function of High School Grades and Aptitude Test Scores
(N = 36,581)

Level of Scores on Academic Aptitude Tests	Average Grade in High School							
	D	C	C+	B−	B	B+	A−	A or A+
11..............						58	71	88
10..............				29	37	56	70	84
9..............			31	34	40	58	69	85
8..............		15	17	33	38	53	71	84
7..............		11	18	30	35	53	73	79
6..............		15	19	22	33	50	70	73
5..............		13	18	24	37	51	64	77
4..............		11	15	23	33	50	57	63
3..............		10	15	20	26	46	53	
2..............		10	13	18	25	42	53	
1..............	4	8	11	15	24	36	40	

Note: Each cell shows the percentage of students who obtained a freshman year average grade of *B* or better, at a given level of aptitude (1–11) and with a given average grade in high school; percentages are not shown for cells which contain less than 50 students.

one finds that the percentages get consistently higher as one goes from the lower to the higher grade averages. In other words, there is a consistent positive relationship between college freshman grades and grades obtained in high school, even when the student's level of academic aptitude is held constant. Correspondingly, if one selects any column of figures and reads up from the bottom, he will find that generally the percentages again increase. Thus, information about the student's scores on tests of academic aptitude is *not* completely redundant with information about his average grade in high school; it can be used to make more accurate the prediction of his academic performance in college.

The data in Table 3 once again underscore the substantial amount of error involved in predicting freshman grades, even when high school grades and aptitude test scores are used in combination. More than 10 percent of the most able students—those with A grades *and* aptitude test scores at the 99th percentile—failed to obtain even a B

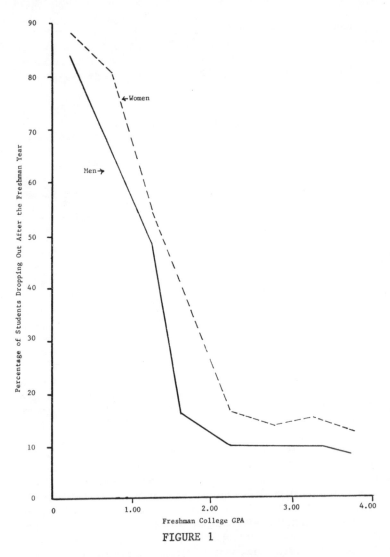

FIGURE 1

Relationship Between Freshman GPA
and Dropping out of College
(N = 36,581 Students)

average during their freshman year in college. Similarly, among students who made only a C average in high school and whose test scores were below the 10th percentile, about 10 percent nevertheless managed to obtain at least a B average.

Predicting Who Will Drop Out

In a very practical sense, the student's ability to stay in college is a more appropriate measure of his "success" than is his freshman GPA. Though good grades will help him to gain admission to graduate school, to be awarded graduate fellowships, and even to secure certain types of jobs, they are irrelevant to any of these outcomes if the student drops out of college before completing his degree requirements. To the admissions officer, then, an understanding of the factors that predict staying in college versus dropping out is at least as important as an understanding of the factors that affect the student's grades.

To investigate the value of high school grades and test scores in predicting the student's chances of dropping out, we utilized the same sample of 36,581 freshmen. A "dropout" was defined as any student who failed to return for his second year of college. Before we performed this analysis, however, it was necessary to examine the relationship between freshman college GPA and dropping out. Figure 1 shows the percentages of men and women within each freshman GPA interval who did not return after the freshman years. As one would expect, the student's chances of dropping out increased as his freshman GPA decreased. Thus, among those freshmen who had A averages, only about one in ten failed to return to college for his sophomore year; by contrast, more than eight in ten of the students with freshman GPAs close to F left college after their first year.

One finding that should be underscored is that the increase in dropouts from one GPA level to the next was not consistent. For example, students with GPAs of C- (1.50) to A (4.00) were relatively unlikely to drop out; but the percentage of dropouts increased precipitously from the C- level on down. (This tendency is indicated in Figure 1 by the lines descending at a very sharp angle and then leveling off almost horizontally. If the relationship between freshman GPA and dropping out were consistent across all grade intervals, the lines would be straight.)

That freshman GPA is related to the student's chances of dropping out is hardly surprising. If the student's freshman grades are poor enough, the college will simply not permit him to stay, even if he wants to. But the relationship between dropping out and freshman GPA did not occur only in the area of failing grades (GPAs from 0.00 to 1.00). On the contrary, the number of dropouts was relatively large for students at the D+ (1.00-1.49) to C- (1.50-2.00) levels. This fact demonstrates that the relationship between dropping out and freshman GPA is not just a result of college regulations governing academic dismissal. Apparently, students whose freshman GPAs are below average (though not failing) are considerably more likely than are students with higher GPAs to decide not to return to college after the freshman year. Some of them may, of course, transfer to other colleges or even return to the same college after a period of time, but the fact remains that they are much less likely to return immediately than are their classmates whose grades are even slightly higher.

One obvious explanation of the marked differences in dropout rates that accompany relatively small differences in freshman GPAs is that students who receive borderline grades become discouraged and so decide not to continue on at the same college. In other words, the student's motivation may be substantially affected by the grades he receives. Another plausible, although not so obvious, interpretation reverses the causal relationship between freshman GPA and dropping out: it is possible that, once the freshman makes up his mind not to return to college for a second year, his motivation to perform well during the remainder of the term suffers. It seems likely that both relationships occur.

Since college GPA is clearly related to dropping out, the same characteristics that predict college GPA should also predict dropping out. The relationship between dropping out and high school grades—the best predictor of freshman GPA—is shown in Table 4.

TABLE 4

Relationship between High School Grades
and Dropping Out of College

(N = 19,524 men and 17,057 women)

Average Grade in High School	Number of Students		Percentage of Students Not Returning for Sophomore Year	
	Men	Women	Men	Women
A or A+............	1,262	1,686	7	12
A−.................	2,035	2,732	8	14
B+.................	3,324	3,893	11	18
B.................	4,247	4,174	17	20
B−.................	3,121	1,982	20	25
C+.................	3,094	1,644	26	28
C.................	2,312	927	33	36
D.................	129	19	47	47

The percentage of dropouts consistently increased as the average grade in high school decreased, though this increase was not nearly as pronounced as in the case of college GPA: fewer than half of the students who had D averages in high school dropped out of college, as compared with more than 80 percent of the students in the lowest interval of freshman GPA. This lower degree of relationship is reflected in the correlation coefficients: college grades correlate -.32 and -.24 with dropping out for men and women, respectively, as compared with correlations of only -.18 and -.16 between high school grades and dropping out.

Does a knowledge of the student's scores on tests of academic ability add anything to our ability to predict his chances of dropping out? In Table 5, we have divided the students into eleven levels of aptitude test scores, separately for each level of high school grades.

TABLE 5

Percentage of Dropouts as a Function of
High School Grades and Aptitude Test Scores

(N = 36,581)

Level of Scores on Academic Aptitude Tests	Average Grade in High School							
	D	C	C+	B−	B	B+	A−	A or A+
11						12	1	6
10					6	6	7	5
9			18	12	13	11	6	7
8		31	19	15	10	13	10	9
7		30	22	17	14	13	12	12
6		26	24	19	15	14	12	12
5		28	23	21	17	15	16	15
4		32	26	20	22	27	28	24
3		35	26	26	23	23	25	
2		33	29	26	26	22	20	
1	48	39	32	30	25	22	28	

Note: Percentages are not shown for cells containing fewer than 50 students.

That a knowledge of the student's test scores, in conjunction with his high school grades, contributes to our ability to predict his dropping out is clear from an inspection of the data. As we proceed down the columns from the highest to the lowest test scores, we find that the student's chances of dropping out increase. (These increases occur in every column, except for students who had average high school grades of C and C+, in which case the percentages do not show the consistent increases found in the other columns.) As a matter of fact, the percentage increases from the highest to the lowest aptitude test levels are just about as large as they are going across the rows from the highest to the lowest grade levels. These trends are reflected in the almost identical correlations of dropping out with the two measures of aptitude: dropping out correlates -.18 and -.17 with aptitude test scores for men and women, respectively, as compared with correlations of -.18 and -.16 with high school grades. Thus, these two measures are about equally useful in predicting whether a student will drop out, in contrast to their effectiveness in predicting freshman GPA, where high school grades carry much more weight than aptitude test scores. The correlations of both of these measures with college grades, however, is considerably higher than their correlations with dropping out. This discrepancy can be seen by comparing Table 5 with Table 3: variations in percentages of students who will get a B average or better range all the way from less than 10 percent to better than 80 percent in Table 3, whereas in Table 5 the percentages go up to only 48. Thus, *even the least able students are more likely to return to college than they are to drop out.*

In summary, these data show that the error involved in using high school grades and test scores to predict who will drop out is even greater than the error involved in predicting the student's freshman GPA.

Effects of the College

So far, we have considered the relationship only of high school grades and test scores to college achievement, independent of the type of college the student attends. In order to see how our predictions are related to the type of college attended, we examined the effects of a large number of institutional characteristics. As it turned out, only one of them—an estimate of the average academic ability of the entering freshman class which we have labeled "selectivity"—had any substantial effects on our predictions. (7) The levels of selectivity are shown in Table 6.

TABLE 6

The Seven Levels of Institutional Selectivity

College Selectivity Level	Number of Institutions	Corresponding Range of Student Mean Scores		
		NMSQT Selection	SAT V + M	ACT Composite
7............	9	129 or higher	1236 or higher	28 or higher
6............	15	121 – 128	1154 – 1235	26 – 27
5............	24	113 – 120	1075 – 1153	25 – 26
4............	44	105 – 112	998 – 1074	23 – 24
3............	45	97 – 104	926 – 997	21 – 22
2............	12	89 – 96	855 – 925	19 – 21
1............	11	88 or lower	854 or lower	18 or lower
No estimate available........	20	88	854	19

To show the true effects of selectivity on college grades, it was necessary to find students attending colleges of differing selectivity who could be "matched" on those attributes that are likely to affect their academic achievement and their persistence in college. To accomplish this end, we searched through our sample of 36,581 to find students who were equated with respect to their high school grades and aptitude test scores but who attended colleges differing in selectivity. Since we could not obtain enough such matches across all seven levels of selectivity to get a reliable picture, we combined the eight selectivity groups (seven levels plus "no estimate available") into three larger categories, as follows:

Broad Selectivity Grouping	Original Selectivity Level
Low	1, 2, and "no estimate"
Medium	3, 4, and 5,
High	6 and 7

In this way, we identified eleven matched groups of students who exist in sufficient number at each of the three levels to permit us to make reliable comparisons. These eleven groups are listed in Table 7. Our criterion for including any group in this analysis was that it must contain at least 50 members attending colleges at each level of selectivity. The first group, for example (average high school grade of A- and aptitude test scores at level 7), was included in our comparisons because at least 50 such students attended colleges at each of the three levels of selectivity. Students with average high school grades of B- and aptitude test scores at level 7, however, were not included because there were only 43 such students attending colleges in the low selectivity category.

TABLE 7

Effects of College Selectivity on the
Student's Freshman Grade-Point Average

(N = 11,368)

Student Group			Percentage Achieving *B* Average or Higher in Colleges of		
Average Grade in High School	Level of Aptitude	N	Low Selectivity	Medium Selectivity	High Selectivity
1. A —	7	962	89	82	62
2. A —	6	692	87	79	55
3. A —	5	538	89	67	46
4. B+	7	1,354	67	62	41
5. B+	6	1,208	76	58	35
6. B+	5	1,105	69	54	32
7. B	7	1,119	60	41	25
8. B	6	1,323	46	35	28
9. B	5	1,471	47	38	27
10. B —	6	681	28	24	15
11. B —	5	915	37	21	24

The data in Table 7 show that as we move from the less to the more selective colleges, there is a steady *decline* in the percentage of students receiving B averages or better during the freshman year. This decline occurs consistently in every group except the last one, where the percentage is slightly greater in the high selectivity group than in the medium group. In short, these data show clearly that the college's *selectivity has a negative effect on the student's freshman GPA.* That is, the more selective the college, the lower a given student's freshmen grades tend to be. That these negative effects are not inconsequential is suggested by the fact that the student's chances of obtaining at least a B average during his freshman year are only about half as great at a highly selective college as at a relatively unselective college.

What do our data on the eleven matched groups suggest with respect to the effects of a college's selectivity on dropping out? Table 8 shows the percentage of dropouts in each of our eleven matched groups, separately for each of the three levels of college selectivity.

TABLE 8

Effects of College Selectivity on the
Student's Chances of Dropping Out

(N = 11,368)

Student Group			Percentage Not Returning after the Freshman Year in Colleges of		
	Average Grade in High School	Level of Aptitude	Low Selectivity	Medium Selectivity	High Selectivity
1.	A—	7	31	12	10
2.	A—	6	18	13	10
3.	A—	5	27	15	14
4.	B+	7	24	16	7
5.	B+	6	28	16	9
6.	B+	5	25	14	12
7.	B	7	33	14	11
8.	B	6	24	16	11
9.	B	5	27	16	14
10.	B—	6	23	21	12
11.	B—	5	27	20	9

Without exception, the dropout rate of each group declines at each increasing level of selectivity. A student attending a college in the low selectivity group, for example, is about two or three times more likely to drop out after his freshman year than is a student of comparable ability attending a highly selective college.

The apparently negative effect of selectivity on dropping out is rather puzzling, particularly when one realizes that the student is likely to get lower grades if he attends the highly selective college. Since students who have below-average freshman GPAs are more likely to drop out than are students with above-average GPAs (Figure 1), it seems to follow that students in the most selective institutions would have higher dropout rates than students of comparable ability enrolled at the least selective institutions. But just the opposite result occurs: a given student is *less* likely to drop out if he attends a highly selective college than if he attends a relatively unselective one, *even though his freshman GPA is likely to be lower at the highly selective college.*

These findings controvert some of the most cherished folklore about the highly selective institution. Some people have suggested, for example, that one of the major liabilities of the more selective institution is that many highly able students who go there find themselves for the first time competing with other students whose intellectual and academic abilities are commensurate with their own; consequently, they become discouraged and drop out. The implication is that certain very bright students would have a better chance of survival at a relatively unselective institution, primarily because the less competitive atmosphere there would permit them to maintain the academic superiority that they had been accustomed to in high school and therefore to avoid the frustration and depression that they may feel in the highly selective institution. Not only do our data fail to support this line of reasoning, but also they suggest that the effect is just the reverse. Furthermore, it holds true for all eleven of our groups; obviously it is not confined to the most able students.

The reason that students are more inclined to leave the less selective colleges after their freshman year is not immediately apparent. Since they obtain higher freshman GPAs than do comparable students in highly selective colleges, they are certainly not asked to leave for academic reasons or because their achievement has not lived up to their own expectations. It is possible that many of them simply transfer to another institution rather than leave college altogether. Freshmen of moderate to high academic ability (which is roughly the span represented by our eleven matched groups) may be disappointed by the low level of competitiveness and of achievement at less selective colleges and may leave, either to seek a more intellectually stimulating environment or (if disillusionment is great enough) to withdraw from higher education altogether, at least for a period of time. Unfortunately, our data provide no direct confirmation of these speculations, which would seem therefore to constitute important topics for future research on college dropouts.

The "Atypical" Student in the Selective College

Many educators criticize the practice of lowering admissions standards for black students on the grounds that these students will be faced with unreasonable academic and social pressures that will greatly increase their chances of dropping out. These personal and academic difficulties are assumed to be especially severe in the most selective institutions.

What do our data show about how the academically "atypical" student performs in the highly selective institution? To arrive at some preliminary answers, we selected several groups of atypical students attending institutions in the top two levels of selectivity (levels 6 and 7). Specifically, six groups (three of men and three of women) were identified on the basis of their having (a) low test scores, (b) low high school grades, or (c) low test scores *and* low high school grades. The comparison of the six groups is shown in Table 9. The first group, for

TABLE 9

Comparison of the Performance of Atypical Students and Typical Students in Highly Selective Colleges[a]

Student Group	N	Percentage Obtaining B Average or Higher in College	Percentage Dropping Out after the Freshman Year
Atypical			
1. Men with average high school grades of C+ or less........	161	14	14
2. Men with aptitude test scores (NMSQT) of 102 or less.....	140	27	9
3. Women with average high school grades of B− or less..	73	22	14
4. Women with aptitude test scores (NMSQT) of 110 or less......................	172	38	9
5. Men with average high school grades of C+ or less *and* aptitude test scores (NMSQT) below 110.................	50	12	12
6. Women with average high school grades of B− or less *and* aptitude test scores (NMSQT) below 110........	24	8	8
Typical			
7. All men in highly selective colleges...................	3,349[b]	41	7
8. All women in highly selective colleges...................	1,857[c]	60	9

[a] All colleges at selectivity levels 6 and 7.
[b] Mean NMSQT score = 130; mean high school grade average = B+.
[c] Mean NMSQT score = 129; mean high school grade average = A −.

example, includes all men enrolled at these highly selective institutions whose high school grades were only C+ or below. Note that, with respect to performance in high school, this group represents the lowest 5 percent of our sample of men attending highly selective institutions (161 out of 3,349). Only 14 percent of the group, as compared with 41 percent of *all* men enrolled in these colleges, obtained B averages or higher in college. If one scans the column of percentages of students who obtained B averages or higher, it becomes clear that each of these atypical groups had freshman GPAs considerably below the average for all students at the highly selective institutions.

However, an examination of the last column in Table 9 reveals that the dropout rates of the atypical students were only slightly higher than the overall dropout rates. In other words, the atypical student at the highly selective college, despite his substantially lower academic performance, is only slightly more inclined than is the typical student to drop out after the freshman year.

These findings have special implications for college admissions policies. First, if a greater number of disadvantaged students are to be admitted under less stringent merit criteria, it is unreasonable to expect that their academic performance will be as high as that of the typical student in the highly selective institution. Using the standard measures of high school grades and test scores, admissions officers and counselors should be able to anticipate fairly accurately just how far below the typical student these specially admitted students will perform. More important, since these atypical students are only slightly more inclined to drop out after the freshman year, *highly selective colleges could admit much larger numbers of students from disadvantaged and atypical backgrounds without substantially increasing their dropout rates.* Once again, these data illustrate the limits of our standard predictors of academic success.

Effects of Race on Performance

The standard admissions criteria are often criticized as being too "culture bound" and therefore not giving a true picture of the academic ability of the typical black student. Recent studies of students attending institutions in the state of Georgia, (8) however, suggest that such may not be the case. This research showed that grades and test scores predicted just as accurately for students attending predominantly black colleges as they did for students attending predominantly white colleges.

Our own data bear more directly on this question. These data were obtained from some 22,000 of the original sample of 36,581 students (9) described earlier. Information concerning students' socioeconomic status, race, and other characteristics was available from a questionnaire administered when the students first entered college in 1966. (10) Our sample included 776 black students, two-thirds of whom were enrolled in predominantly Negro colleges.

In order to test the appropriateness of the standard merit criteria separately for students of different races, we established three different groups: black students attending black colleges, black students attending white colleges, and white (11) students attending

TABLE 10

Mean High School Grades, Aptitude Test Scores, and College Selectivity for Six Groups of Students

	Men			Women		
	Whites in White Colleges	Blacks in White Colleges	Blacks in Black Colleges	Whites in White Colleges	Blacks in White Colleges	Blacks in Black Colleges
Mean freshman GPA						
Actual...................	2.35	2.08	2.23	2.56	2.13	2.20
Estimated...............	2.35	2.14	2.26	2.56	2.33	2.32
Percentage dropping out after the freshman year						
Actual...................	12.4	7.4	12.7	13.9	20.3	13.3
Estimated...............	12.3	14.3	13.2	13.7	23.9	13.3

[a] Based on the students' high school grades, aptitude test scores, and college selectivity.

TABLE 11

Actual and Estimated[a] Freshman GPAs and Dropout Rates for Six Groups of Students

(N = 1,047 men and 1,021 women)

	Men			Women		
	Whites in White Colleges	Blacks in White Colleges	Blacks in Black Colleges	Whites in White Colleges	Blacks in White Colleges	Blacks in Black Colleges
Mean freshman GPA						
Actual.............	2.35	2.08	2.23	2.56	2.13	2.20
Estimated..........	2.35	2.14	2.26	2.56	2.33	2.32
Percentage dropping out after the freshman year						
Actual.............	12.4	7.4	12.7	13.9	20.3	13.3
Estimated..........	12.3	14.3	13.2	13.7	23.9	13.3

[a] Based on the students' high school grades, aptitude test scores, and college selectivity.

white colleges. (The number of white students attending black colleges was too small to permit valid comparisons.) Each of these three groups was further categorized by sex, making a total of six groups. To reduce computing costs, we used 10 percent random samples of the two groups of white students (men and women) rather than the total groups (which numbered about 10,000 students each). Test scores, high school grades, and college selectivity for each of the six groups are shown in Table 10.

We first selected a random sample (1,047 men and 1,021 women) of *all* students without regard to their race or institution. Regression equations for predicting freshman GPA were developed for each sex, using the students' high school grades, aptitude test scores, and college selectivity since, as we have seen, selectivity is an important factor in affecting freshman grades. The regression weights obtained from the two analyses based on all students were then applied separately to the students in each of the six samples (three groups of men and three of women), in order to arrive at an "estimated" or "predicted" freshman GPA and probability of dropping out. Table 11 compares (a) the mean estimated freshman GPAs with the mean actual freshman GPAs and (b) the estimated percentage of dropouts with the actual percentage of dropouts for each of the six groups. The average estimated GPA for the two samples of white students are almost identical with their actual GPAs—a finding which is to be expected since white students comprised the bulk of the sample from which the initial weights were derived. However, for all four samples of black students, the estimated grades are slightly *higher* than the actual grades obtained by these students in their freshman year. The differences are small among the men, and somewhat larger among women, particularly black women attending white colleges.

These findings show that black students, particularly women, perform slightly below what would be expected on the basis of their high school grades and aptitude test scores. This overprediction obtains, regardless of whether the black student attends a predominantly black or a predominantly white college. In short, the traditional admissions criteria, far from discriminating against black students, favor them somewhat, in that they overpredict slightly how well the students will do academically during the freshman year.

The data on predicting dropouts (Table 11) give a similar picture: in general, the predicted and actual percentages are very close. It is of interest, however, that the dropout rates among black students attending white colleges are slightly *below* the rate that would be expected from their test scores, high school grades, and college selectivity. Although only the discrepancy for men is statistically significant ($p < .05$), these differences suggest some provocative speculations. Perhaps the typical black student attending a white college receives special tutoring and counseling that reduces his chance of dropping out, or perhaps he is simply more determined to succeed, because of the exceptional situation in which he finds himself, than is the typical white student in these colleges. Whatever the true explanation, it is again clear that the dropout rate of the predominantly white college will probably not be greatly affected if its enrollment of black students is substantially increased.

Are Admission Practices "Racist"?

Critics of current admissions practices correctly assume that the low proportion of Negroes among the students entering many of the more selective institutions is caused in part by the use of test scores and grades in admissions. Whether this *de facto* segregation of the races is evidence of "racist" attitudes on the part of these institutions, however, is another matter. Racism has to do with intention: if admissions officers apply merit criteria in a conscious and deliberate attempt to exclude black students, then the charge of racism seems valid. On the other hand, if segregation turns out to be an unintended by-product of the application of merit criteria, then the charge seems groundless.

Although a discussion of possible racist motives on the part of higher educational institutions may seem tangential to the topic of this paper, it is important to recognize that such arguments are frequently raised in discussions of admissions procedures. That *de facto* segregation among entering freshman classes is not a sufficient basis for concluding that racist motives are operating can be seen by examining other fields where merit is the primary criterion for admission. Two such areas are professional sports and jazz. It is well known that the proportions of Negroes in these two fields are much higher than their proportion in the population. But is it valid to conclude that this overrepresentation is a consequence of "racist" attitudes on the part of the persons who control access to these fields? Are whites discriminated against in screening candidates for these professions? Is favoritism shown toward blacks? Such conclusions would seem to be highly untenable, particularly in the case of professional sports where, until recently, blacks were excluded altogether. The overrepresentation of blacks in professional basketball and football is all the more remarkable when one realizes that most of the professionals in these two sports come from the ranks of college graduates. Negroes comprise less than 4 percent of all college graduates, (12) and yet they account for more than one-fourth of all professional football and basketball players. In short, then, one cannot infer that disproportionate representation of the races in a particular field of endeavor is evidence of racist attitudes on the part of the persons responsible for deciding who shall be admitted. Depending upon the field, a certain degree of disproportionality may result from the blind application of merit criteria without reference to race or color.

In some respects, it is ironic that the merit system of admissions has been attacked by persons concerned with equal rights and equal educational opportunity. As Jencks and Riesman (13) have pointed out, one remarkable feature of the American system of higher education during the past fifty years is its transition from a basically aristocratic system—one in which social class and family influence were the primary determinants of college attendance—to a fundamentally meritocratic system, in which people are admitted on the basis of what they can do rather than who they are.

Many colleges have tried to correct *de facto* segregation by abandoning or modifying the merit criterion so as to include a higher proportion of black students among their entering classes. One of the difficulties with such programs is that they are often administered covertly as "special programs for the disadvantaged," suggesting that their proponents still implicitly accept the merit criterion as the prime consideration in admissions.

Another problem is that the rationale for special admissions programs has never been clearly enunciated and defended by its advocates. Essentially, the introduction of such programs implies that a new value has taken precedence over the traditional one of merit. The proponents of double standards in admissions are in essence arguing that achieving a better racial balance in the student body is a more important objective than blindly applying a criterion based purely on merit. It seems to me that, given the increased racial tensions and the pressures for black separatism that have developed lately, a strong case could be made for this point of view.

In addition to expanding educational opportunities, increasing the extent of racial integration in colleges can be defended on the pragmatic grounds that, in the long run, it would tend to promote racial understanding and thereby to reduce the likelihood of racial violence. An anonymous person of a different color is much easier to hate or vilify than is a friend, associate, or neighbor, regardless of what his color might be. In this regard, the move within some colleges to establish separate curricula, dormitories, and social organizations for blacks seems to defeat the goal of promoting communication and understanding between the races by admitting more black students.

Maintaining "Academic Standards"

Opponents commonly raise the objection that even partial abandonment of the merit criterion in admissions would result in a lowering of the "academic standards" of the institution. While such a consequence is indeed possible, it is by no means inevitable. Part of the folklore of higher education is that academic standards are determined primarily by the abilities of the students who are admitted. This bit of folklore may apply to certain institutions that grade strictly "on the curve," but there is no reason why colleges cannot set any standards they wish, independent of their admissions practices. Standards have to do with the performance levels that the institution demands before it will certify that the student has passed certain courses or completed certain requirements for the degree. It is true that fewer students are likely to succeed ("be certified") if very high performance standards are maintained at the same time that admissions criteria are relaxed. Nevertheless, standards of performance can still be defined and maintained, whatever changes are made in the admissions process.

The problem of certification relates closely to the issue of *absolute* versus *relative* standards of performance in higher education. One difficulty with the grading systems used in American colleges is their relativity: an A grade at one institution may not be comparable to an A at another institution. Some of the more selective colleges apparently adjust certification standards to reflect their students' high absolute level of performance: the average freshman GPA in the most selective colleges is about 0.50 higher than the average GPA in the least selective. (14) Not all institutions and professors make such adjustments, however, so that a student *of a given level of ability* has a better chance of obtaining an A grade at an unselective college than at a highly selective one (Table 7). In view of such erratic grading practices, it is easy to see why graduate schools, employers, and others rely on admissions standards in judging the *academic* standards of the institution: admission criteria—in particular, average scores of entering students on standardized tests—represent objective measures which permit valid comparisons among institutions. The higher the admissions standards, the higher (presumably) the academic standards. Clearly, admissions standards would not have to be used in this manner if institutions had absolute (that is, comparable), rather than relative, standards of performance.

Educating Students or Picking Winners?

In my judgment, *the model of selective admissions based on test scores and grades is inappropriate for institutions of higher education.* Presumably, educational institutions exist in order to educate students. Their mission, then, is to produce certain desirable *changes* in the student or, more simply, to make a difference in the student's life. Given these goals, they should strive in their admissions practices to select those applicants who are most likely to be favorably influenced by the particular educational program offered at the institution. Instead, the typical admissions officer today functions more like a handicapper: he tries merely to pick winners. He looks over the various candidates, evaluates their respective talents, and attempts to select those who are most likely to perform well. Handicappers, it should be stressed, are interested only in *predicting* the horse's performance—not in improving his performance, in trying to make him run better and faster. The problem here is that an educational institution is supposed to function less like a handicapper and more like a jockey or a trainer: it has a responsibility to *improve the performance* of the individual, not just to identify those with the greatest potential.

In another sense, college admissions officers have tended to operate like personnel managers in a commercial enterprise rather than like educators. Picking winners is an appropriate activity for businesses and industries, since their goal is to hire the very best talent so as to maximize productivity and profit. Similarly, competition among rival companies for the limited pool of available talent is consistent with the very nature of business. This business model, however—though it seems to have been adopted by many institutions—is not appropriate for education. The mission of the college is *not* simply to maximize its output of distinguished alumni by maximizing its input of talented students. Such a static view puts the college in the role of a kind of funnel, where what comes out is purely a matter of what goes in. Colleges and other educational institutions exist in order to *change* the student, to contribute to his personal development, to *make a difference*. Whereas the personnel manager is looking for applicants who can help the company, the admissions officer *should* be looking for applicants who can be helped by the institution.

That colleges are basically more interested in picking winners than in improving the student's performance is revealed by the rationale usually given for using high school grades and test scores in admissions. Institutions typically justify the application of these merit criteria on the grounds that they predict subsequent academic performance in college. Thus, applicants with poor grades and low test scores are not admitted because they are less likely to perform well than are students with high grades and high test scores. In short, the highly able student is admitted not because he has demonstrated greater potential for growth or change than the less able student, but simply because his achievement is likely to be higher.

Unfortunately, little is known about how to identify those students who are most likely to benefit from particular types of educational programs. But it is entirely possible that the character of student bodies would change radically if *potential for change* replaced academic aptitude as the principal criterion of merit in college admissions. It is not inconceivable, for example, that the very brightest students will achieve at a high level, no matter where they attend college. Thus, they may have very low potential for being benefited educationally by institutions; they would perform just as well in relatively unstructured situations where the only facilities were, say, a good library. Some of the less able applicants, on the other hand, may be highly susceptible to the influence of the college environment. The point here is that, with respect to making a difference in the performance of their students, many institutions may be squandering their resources by admitting only the brightest among their applicants.

Another argument frequently given to support the use of the standard merit criteria is that only the brightest students are capable of "profiting" from higher education. Presumably, this argument implicitly accepts the rationale for higher education just discussed: potential for *change* should be the principal basis for admissions. Recent evidence, however, fails to support this assumption, since students at all levels of ability showed similar gains in achievement during their undergraduate years, regardless of the type of institution they attended. (15)

Still another justification for using the standard merit criteria in admissions relates to the use of college admissions as a form of *reward*. Many parents, teachers, and students view being admitted to college as a kind of recognition for past achievement. This concept confuses the certification and the admissions functions. Clearly, it is appropriate for institutions to reward high achievement at the time of certification; but to treat the admissions decision as a kind of prize for good performance in high school is to distort the admissions function and, hence, the mission of the institution.

In short, the use of the college admissions process to "pick winners" is not consistent with the *educational* mission of the institution. what seems to be needed is a serious re-examination of the entire rationale for admissions and increased research to assist each college in identifying those students who are most likely to benefit from its particular educational program. In this way, institutions can better fulfill their responsibilities to both the individual and the society.

Race as a Criterion in Admissions

Defenders of the merit system in admissions may argue that applying different admissions standards to different races is basically unfair and discriminatory. While there is truth in this argument, it should be pointed out that colleges have for years been willing on occasion to subordinate merit to other criteria in admissions, with very little outcry from the proponents of the merit system. The practice that immediately comes to mind in this connection is the use of sex quotas—the most extreme form being the single-sex college. Other forms of discrimination include setting higher merit standards for out-of-state applicants to public institutions, lowering merit standards for athletes and for the children of alumni, and varying merit standards for different regions (a device used by some selective institutions to achieve a "geographic mix"). With the possible exception of lowering standards for athletes, these discriminatory admissions practices have seldom been criticized as compromising the merit criterion. The point is simply that an acceptable rationale—either moral or educational—can be and has been made for waiving the merit criterion in favor of other criteria in the admissions process. If racial quotas are to be given precedence to merit criteria, it is imperative that the advocates of such quotas make their case immediately and convincingly.

Even if most colleges were to adopt racial quotas in their admissions policies, however, it is unlikely that a satisfactory degree of racial integration in student bodies could be achieved. The fundamental problem here is that there are simply too few black students in the total pool of college-bound students. A concerted effort by all predominantly white colleges to recruit more black students may serve simply to redistribute the inadequate pool that now exists. (16) Since most white institutions would probably apply the standard merit criteria within their black applicant group, their increased recruitment efforts might conceivably have a "trickling down" effect in that many predominantly black colleges would be forced to find new students to replace those recruited by the predominantly white colleges. It is doubtful whether these institutions have either the resources or the drawing power to identify and recruit substantial numbers of new students from among the non-college-bound population.

The point here is that competing for candidates within the pool of college-bound students has little effect on the size of the total pool. Clearly, what is needed is a much more concentrated effort on the part of colleges and universities to recruit many more black students from among those who might otherwise not attend college.

With respect to the broader social problem of racial tension, the importance of increasing the pool of black students attending colleges can hardly be overestimated. Consider, for example, that we live in a society where education, particularly higher education, is increasingly a prerequisite for entry into most of the higher status and higher paid professions. Consider also that one of the prime sources of racial tension is the reality that most blacks live in less affluent circumstances than most whites. If higher education is one of the principal avenues of escape from poverty and from ghetto life, then the current representation of blacks among college freshmen (6-7 percent) must be considered woefully inadequate. In short, we have a situation where the typical black is already far behind the typical white economically and where he is sure to fall still further behind because his chances of obtaining a higher education are substantially less than the white's chances.

Given the current economic chasm between blacks and whites, one could argue that the proportion of blacks going on to higher education should, for a period of time, be even *greater* than the proportion of whites. Instead, we have a situation where the economic gap is likely to widen with time. The undesirable social consequences that are likely to result from this increasing discrepancy can be avoided only if higher educational institutions are prepared to undertake major crash programs that will greatly increase the proportion of black students who go on to college. Simply stealing some other college's black students will not do the job. Individual institutions must make an intensive effort to intervene at the secondary school level with programs designed to encourage black students to go to college. While such programs present many educational, economic, and logistical problems, these are minor compared with the increased racial tension that is likely to accompany a widening in the socioeconomic gap that already exists between the races.

Institutional Responsibility for Specially-Admitted Students

A question which is still far from settled is how much responsibility for the student's progress the institution assumes when it admits him—frequently after active recruiting efforts—under merit criteria substantially below those used in admitting most other students. Should he simply be left to sink or swim as other students are? Should he be offered special programs of tutoring, remedial work, and counseling? If so, how should these programs be designed? How are they to be financed? How is the student ultimately to be assimilated into the regular academic program?

More important is the question of academic standards. Should the specially admitted black student be required to perform at the same level as other students if he is to receive academic credit for given courses and to earn a degree? It is likely that some concerned professors and administrators will be tempted to apply lower standards in evaluating the performance of black students so as to enhance their apparent level of achievement and thereby reduce their chances of academic failure and disappointment. While such double standards may have some desirable temporary effects—such as higher student morale and less institutional guilt—in the long run they would probably encourage the development of racist policies. Employers, graduate schools, and professional schools, for example, would want to know whether the students had earned a "black degree" or a "white degree." Such problems, which are inherent in any system that employs double standards of performance, highlight the need for differentiating clearly between *admissions* standards and *performance* standards.

Conclusions

In this paper, we have examined certain alternative arguments concerning college admissions policies and racial problems. We have attempted to explore some of the basic assumptions involved in the use of aptitude test scores and high school grades in college admissions and to present recent empirical evidence concerning the relative usefulness of these measures for students of different races. Our analysis and discussion seem to warrant the following conclusions:

1) The low representation of blacks among entering college freshmen and the *de facto* racial segregation that exists in many colleges is attributable in part to the use, in the admissions process, of high school grades and, in particular, of scores on tests of academic ability. As predictors of the individual student's chances of success in college, test scores and school grades are subject to considerable error. Thus, other criteria could probably be employed in the admissions process with only minor unfavorable effects on the level of academic performance and on the dropout rate.

2) Black students—whether they attend white or black colleges—on the average perform academically at the level that would be predicted from their high school grades and test scores. (The average performance of black women is slightly below expectation.) Dropout rates of black students attending white colleges, however, are slightly *lower* than is predicted from grades and test scores.

3) The goal of furthering racial integration in colleges basically conflicts with the use of purely meritocratic standards in admissions. If merit considerations in admissions are to be successfully subordinated to racial considerations, then the case for integration and increased educational opportunities for blacks needs to be made convincingly.

4) Predominantly white colleges that lower their admissions standards (with respect to required grades and test scores) so as to admit more black students are not likely to experience significant changes in their dropout rates, although the college grades of these specially admitted students will tend to be lower than the grades of other students.

5) A basic problem in attempting to achieve a higher degree of racial integration in American colleges is that the total supply of black college-bound youth is inadequate. Competing for students within this pool is not likely to increase the size of the pool. If significantly more integration is to be achieved, individual colleges must make a greater attempt to encourage non-college-bound black students to attend college.

6) The lowering of *admissions* standards does not necessarily result in the lowering of academic standards. In theory, at least, institutions are free to set standards of performance independently of their admissions standards. A major obstacle here is that peformance standards (grades) are relative rather than absolute. The use of absolute standards of performance—which

would be comparable across institutions—would obviate the need to rely on admissions standards (average test scores) in assessing the "academic excellence" of the institution.

7) American colleges have pursued the use of meritocratic criteria in admissions so vigorously that the *educational* mission of the institution has become blurred. "Picking winners" may be appropriate for businesses and other enterprises that are primarily interested in exploiting talent, but it is an inappropriate model for institutions that exist to influence or *change* those people who are selected. Thus, the principal purpose of the admissions process should be to select the students who are most likely to benefit from the institution's educational program. Since recent research indicates that the most highly able students are not necessarily those who can be the most changed by the college experience, much more research on the problem of how to identify students with high potential for change is needed.

Notes

(1) John A. Creager et al., *National Norms for Entering College Freshmen—Fall 1968* (Washington: Office of Research, American Council on Education, 1968). In response to a question about racial background, 5.8 percent checked "Negro." "Negro." Since we have evidence that some Negro students preferred to check "Other" in response to this question, the 5.8 percent is something of an underestimate. It is very unlikely, however, that Negro students who did not check "Negro" account for more than 1 percent of all students.

(2) Alexander W. Astin, Robert J. Panos, and John A. Creager, *National Norms for Entering College Freshmen—Fall 1966* (Washington: Office of Research, American Council on Education, 1967). Robert J. Panos, Alexander W. Astin, and John A. Creager, *National Norms for Entering College Freshmen—Fall 1967* (Washington: Office of Research, American Council on Education, 1967).

(3) Even this statistic is misleading: most predominantly Negro colleges enroll virtually no white students; at a few colleges—located mostly in the border states—whites constitute nearly half of the student body and thus raise the overall average.

(4) Alan E. Bayer and Robert F. Boruch, *The Black Student in American Colleges* (Washington: Office of Research, American Council on Education, 1969).

(5) John R. Hills, "Use of Measurement in Selection and Placement," in R. L. Thorndike, ed., *Educational Measurement,* 2nd ed. (Washington, D. C.: American Council on Education, 1971), pp. 680-732. David E. Lavin, *The Prediction of Academic Performance: A Theoretical Analysis and Review of Research* (New York: Russell Sage Foundation, 1965).

(6) Alexander W. Astin, *Predicting Academic Performance in College* (New York: Free Press, 1971).

(7) Separate regression analyses were also carried using only institutions *within* each level of selectivity. In general, the predictive accuracy of test scores and high school grades was very similar at each level (see Astin, *Predicting Academic Performance in College,* for details).

(8) J. C. Stanley and A. C. Porter, "Correlation of Scholastic Aptitude Test Score with College Grades for Negroes Versus Whites," *Journal of Educational Measurement* 4, no. 4 (1967).

(9) These 22,000 students included all of those from the original sample of 36,581 students who returned a follow-up questionnaire mailed out in the summer of 1967.

(10) Astin et al., *National Norms—Fall 1966.*

(11) These "white" students might be more accurately termed "nonblack," since they include all who checked an alternative other than "Negro" on the racial background item (Caucasian, Oriental, American Indian, Other). However, since

more than 90 percent of this group checked "Caucasian," we have used the term "white" rather than the awkward "nonblack."

(12) Alexander W. Astin and Robert J. Panos, *The Educational and Vocational Development of College Students* (Washington: American Council on Education, 1969).

(13) Christopher Jencks and David Riesman, *The Academic Revolution* (Garden City, N. Y.: Doubleday & Co., 1968).

(14) Astin, *Predicting Academic Performance in College.*

(15) Alexander W. Astin, *The College Environment* (Washington: American Council on Education, 1968).

(16) It should be stressed that the underrepresentation of blacks among entering college freshmen (6-7 percent versus 12 percent in the college-age population) is in part the result of high dropout rates among blacks in high school: only about 10 percent of the high school graduates are black. *Current Population Reports,* Population Characteristics, Series P-20, No. 182, April 28, 1969; "Educational Attainment: March, 1968."

III

Experiences
of Black College Students
at Predominantly
White Institutions

James M. Hedegard

Much is currently being written on the problems surrounding the expansion of opportunities for higher education to include larger numbers of blacks. Some of this discusses what it is like to be a black student. Most is, however, anecdotal. Little systematically examines both the individual's spectrum of experiences and the variety among black students. The purpose here is to examine some of the research which at least attempts systematic inquiry.

Several of the more systematic studies of black students focus on a single institution. (1) A few others look at students' experiences in a number of institutions. (2) Studies which focus on a single institution do not permit a clear separation of the experiences contingent on characteristics of the particular school and those to be more generally expected. Also, single institutions enroll students in idiosyncratic ways, perhaps especially in opportunity-expanding programs, such as those designed for black students. Thus, no single school's black student population is at all a cross section of potential black college students (still less is it a cross section of the black age cohort).

What is the most useful purpose that a discussion such as this can serve? One answer might be to describe the experiences that black students have. Another might be to describe the experiences that "being black" add to those of "being a student." At present, we can provide significant information regarding experiences, at least for some black students at some institutions. We are not in a good position to determine the particular effects of color on the students' position; we can only suggest, hypothesize, part of the answer.

Why cannot we produce a good answer to the question of the unique impacts of "being black"? Part of the answer is, of course, that we have only a scattering of available data. Even if we had good data, however, it is not clear how we could isolate "being black" from the various other characteristics of college students. For example, the black and white student populations, especially at more selective colleges and universities, differ systematically on a variety of characteristics not necessarily associated with race (e.g. parents' income, education, and values; academic and career plans; patterns of pre-college activities and experience; pre-college academic achievement; perhaps basic political and social beliefs, and others). One research strategy to facilitate the examination of the impact of "being black" on a student's experiences, goals, etc., has involved matching blacks and whites on characteristics known to predict to the experiences and goals under study. Black and white students can be matched on (a) pre-college academic achievement, as measured by various tests such as the SAT or ACT batteries, (b) socioeconomic status, as measured by parents' education, income, job level, and (c) major goals for attending college, along dimensions such as vocational–academic or instrumental–academic.

In some selective institutions this matching is hard to achieve, as there may be very little overlap between the distributions of blacks and whites on the matching characteristic. Even when such matchings can be achieved (and I know of no comprehensive study of student experiences in which students were matched on all of the above three sets of variables) the question can be asked: what does the matching mean? For example, in what sense are white and black families matched on socioeconomic class, in terms of equating students' pre-college experiences and environments.

To turn this coin over, perhaps we should not be concerned with matching. If our goal is to maximize the opportunities for persons to get the kinds of education that will help them achieve their goals and best utilize their abilities, then studying black students who are from working-class families and have relatively low pre-college academic achievement will tell us something of their stresses, as well as those which non-black students with the same pre-college experiences and achievements have. Or at least it may sensitize us to possible stresses. And, educational opportunity and success are not uniform across the white population. (3)

Given these considerations, the primary focus here is on the experiences of black students at predominantly white colleges and universities, whether or not these experiences are shared with numbers of whites. Where data permit, differences among identifiably dissimilar groups of black students will be examined. These include differences in the socioeconomic class of the family, and variations among students who differ on basic goals to be served by the college experience. Further, some comparisons will be made between whites and blacks who are matched on certain characteristics.

The Freshman Experience

The black college students' experiences will be examined in two parts: first, the students' experiences in the freshman year; second, the students' overall experiences viewed from later in their college careers, especially as viewed by students nearing graduation. This is done for two reasons. First, the vast literature on changes in college students' beliefs and characters strongly suggests that the college experience has its greatest impact in the freshman year (as do seniors' retrospective reports of college problems and stresses). (4) Second, seniors are a non-random subgroup of entering students who, through various selection processes, have survived in academia. The perceptions of these "survivors" can provide valuable insights about black-white interaction at a large university.

At many colleges and universities, entering black students can be placed into two groups: 1) regularly-admitted black students, who tend to come from college-oriented urban and suburban high schools, tend to be from middle-class or upper-working-class homes, who have a range of academic and career goals comparable to the range of their fellow white students, and who evidence (via admissions tests and high school performance) academic preparation comparable to that of other incoming students; 2) specially-admitted black students, who tend to come from predominantly black urban high schools, who are predominantly from working-class families with per capita incomes far below those of the modal white students, who tend at admission to view college strongly as a place for vocational preparation, and who evidence pre-college academic achievement near the bottom of the range of achievement evidenced by white students at the same school. What research there is available on the experiences of black students has focused more on the latter group. (5) Some data do exist on samples of regularly-admitted blacks. (6) A few studies do not specify the social origins of their sampled black students. (7)

The discussion which follows will focus on studies of specially-admitted students at the University of Michigan who completed batteries of questionnaires just prior to and toward the end of their first university year. Some hypotheses will be drawn about the freshman experiences of regularly-admitted black students but these are only conjectures.

First a word on the student samples. The Opportunity Award program at the University of Michigan was designed to increase opportunity for college study. The students admitted into the university via the program are those who appear capable of academic success at the university but who require special assistance and financial aid. Nominations for the program are generally made by secondary school principals or counselors. Although selection is not restricted to Negroes, to date most students recruited have been black. These students tend to have Scholastic Aptitude Test (SAT) scores in the lower portion of the distribution for all incoming students. Many, though, ranked academically near the top of their high school classes. In high school these students were often labelled and rewarded by their high school teachers as "students" and tended to label themselves as such on the Coleman typology (alternative labels being "athlete, "activity leader," etc.). Compared with the more modal white students, these students reported somewhat less active encouragement and prodding toward academic success from their parents. Although most initially planned to study in the liberal arts and science areas, their personal goals and plans looked more like those of nursing and engineering students than like those of traditional liberal arts students. In fact, along with some of the whites, several of the women students moved into nursing later on, and a number of both men and women moved into education fields. (8) Several schools appear to specially recruit black students in a similar fashion. This sample probably matches closely a large portion of the black student population at other somewhat selective schools.

Upon arrival at the university, a number of the black students admitted under the Opportunity Award program experienced intense feelings of loneliness and isolation. They found themselves among whites, perhaps with a white roommate, many having scarcely met whites prior to college. A few fared better, arriving with black friends or already knowing blacks on campus.

In contrast, several of the regularly admitted black students arrived with white high-school classmates. A few already knew the campus well, having lived nearby or having known students already at the university.

Many, especially the women, found their encounters with whites to be superficial and frustrating. Some experienced outright hostility. Others experienced (and possibly contributed to) wariness and mistrust. Neither whites nor blacks could deliver the closeness and concern which the initial contacts seemed to promise. Among a number of the working-class black women this sense of isolation was only eased when they joined one of the black sororities. Contributing to this sense of isolation was the difficulty experienced by a number of black women in obtaining dates. On the whole, black men had an easier time of dating, and several of the black women were quite angry at the black men who dated white women. (9)

Another, perhaps more serious, problem for specially-admitted freshman blacks was meeting the academic demands of the university. Most blacks expected to do slightly less well in their courses than did white students. On the average, their grades were even lower than they expected. Some had to reduce their course loads in midterm, due to overall poor performance. One student, viewing the academic difficulties she and her friends were experiencing, was driven to wonder whether blacks might indeed be intellectually inferior to whites. Along with disappointing grades went a number of incidental and scattered experiences. Several students said they were unremittingly criticized for mistakes in speech and writing. Others reported being constantly wrong when responding to instructors' questions. Still others felt badgered and hunted down in class to expose their ignorance. Of course, some of the black students had the opposite kinds of experiences. They were much relieved to do better in courses than they expected and gained a good deal of confidence in the process. Many found at least one concerned and understanding instructor, who took time to work with them individually. (10)

Several students reported their major academic problem to be learning to think within the abstract and conceptual frameworks which characterized college courses and that, once they had learned to do this, academic work became much easier. Upon entrance, blacks had, by-and-large, more concrete and tangible views of, and preferences for objects in, the world than entering freshmen generally.

As with many students, the freshman (and sophomore) year was a watershed for the selection of an academic field and, in some cases, for a career. Some students found the first course required for their major (for example, introductory chemistry) an absolute stopper. Plans had to be changed right there. Other students found the introductory work at the college level to be quite unlike their high school work in the same field (for example, the first college mathematics course).

Our data suggest a secondary effect of the difficulty of meeting academic demands. To meet academic demands, a number of these black students had to study extremely hard and had to cut back rather far their usual range of college activities.

Like many whites, a number of black students became more academically oriented and less directly vocationally oriented during their first year. Perhaps part of this was due to an acceptance of the goals embodied in the curriculum. Another factor might be the necessity to invest oneself heavily in the immediately academic simply to pass through college successfully.

By-and-large, these black students were less satisfied with the experiences and achievements of their freshman year, than were their white counterparts. However, the difference here was not striking. There was considerable overlap between the two distributions. As on each of the above points, there was a considerable range of overall evaluations among the black students.

Our study focused on the post-freshman year experience and did not look closely at student perceptions of the university as an institution at the end of this first year. (11) Issues between black students and the university were not prominent during this year (1966-1967). They did become prominent as these students became juniors and seniors and the following is a look at their impacts.

The Overall College Experience

Black students experience college (and themselves) in widely differing ways. Even in their experiencing "being black," in experiencing the attitudes of whites toward them, and in their perceptions of the posture and intentions of the university in its various dealings with blacks, there is virtually a full spectrum of possible opinion and response among black students. (12)

Looking first at experiences bearing on "being black" and black-white relations in some detail, the modal black experience of fellow white students is that they are ignorant of and indifferent to the problems and experiences of blacks. A less frequent reaction accuses white students of outright bigotry and prejudice. On the other hand, some blacks have had very different experiences, and report that white students with whom they have had significant contact are tolerant and understanding. But this is a minority perception. There is a similar spread of blacks' reactions to contact with faculty members. As mentioned in the previous section on the freshman experiences, many black students encounter early very frustrating classroom criticism, even failure. Some interpreted this as "racist" in motivation, although the same kinds of experiences are reported by a number of white students, especially by white students from working-class homes. The experience of racism stems from a variety of kinds of classroom experience: 1) being prejudged as inferior or inadequately prepared for academic work; 2) being constantly criticized for forms and style of speech and writing; 3) being singled out for criticism, such as being constantly called upon by an instructor who knows the student will be unprepared; 4) feeling that papers, exams, are downgraded for irrelevant reasons; 5) feeling classroom pressures to become intellectual, or middle-class, or white. (13) These experiences are some unknown combination of prejudice, hostility, and indifference on the part of instructors, and projection and a denial of inadequacy on the part of the students. Students cited some incidents which seem bonafide instances of bigotry and prejudgment on the part of faculty. A few faculty have spoken of nearly drastic consequences of their own prejudgment of black students. Other instances cited seem clearly not racist in the sense of bigotry and prejudgment.

Black students' reactions to instructors and their total classroom experiences seem more moderate, or better modulated, than their overall reactions to white students, on the whole. If this in fact is a correct inference, perhaps it reflects the fact that, generally, students are more dependent upon each other than they are on instructors.

In contrast to black students' reactions to their experiences with white students, a high proportion of white students in various studies report themselves becoming more tolerant, understanding, sympathetic, and concerned about black students and their problems. (14)

Black students' reactions to the university, as a sort of corporate policy-making and executive body, also vary. In the study at Michigan (15) black and white seniors were interviewed immediately after a black-university controversy and a student strike over programs to increase black opportunity at the university. Most black students were quite angry at the university. Some felt it had been indifferent to black demands for marked increases in numbers of black students, the hiring of more black staff, greater financial aid, etc. Others felt the university was determined not to accede to those demands. However, even with this heated confrontation in the immediate past, a few black students felt the university had been more than conciliatory, perhaps overly responsive to the pressures put on it by black students and white friends.

Our interview data suggest that black-institution confrontations can politicize black students, at least for the short haul. This occurred for at least two reasons: 1) some black students were surprised at what they saw to be the university's intransigence; 2) carrying out the black action accompanying the demands and negotiation required a temporary organization, working together, administrative skills, etc. which brought some black students into contact with each other for the first time, working for a common cause, and successfully exercising and testing previously untried talents and skills.

The overall academic experiences of black students seem continuous with their first year academic experiences. The graduating seniors are a select subgroup of the entering freshmen. At the University of Michigan a number of the specially-admitted black students do drop from the program, although the majority continue on to graduate in four or five years, and succeeding entering groups have higher and higher percentages of students continuing through to degrees. Despite some schools' claims that, once socialized into the various role demands of college students, black students' academic performance "takes off" to attain levels above those attained by white students of the same level of measured academic achievement at entrance, two studies suggest this is not the case. We compared the academic performance of pairs of black and white students matched on SAT scores at entrance and on planned major fields of study. Our sample included most of the specially-admitted black students who entered the University of Michigan in the fall of 1966. Our preliminary analyses suggest that the academic performances of the black and white members of these pairs is quite similar. If anything, the white members of the pairs are more likely to experience academic success than the blacks. Where students do "take off" academically (we assessed "taking off" by comparing students later grade-point averages, in terms 5, 6, and 7, with those attained earlier in terms 2, 3, and 4, and called "taking off" a rise in average GPA of .50 or more) it appeared usually to be the result of moving into a more congenial field of study rather than of suddenly catching hold in a field originally chosen. And only a minority of students do "take off" according to these standards. A team of researchers from the Educational Testing Service obtained somewhat parallel findings. They examined the relationship between students' SAT scores at entrance to college and their GRE scores as seniors for each of a number of black and white colleges. On the whole, the various schools generated quite similar regression lines. There were some differences among colleges in slope and elevation of these lines, but slope and elevation did not distinguish black from white colleges. (16)

A number of black students are no longer in the university as seniors. As always in studying attrition, it is hard to determine exactly what happened to them, and why. Some moved to other schools (urban universities, community colleges, technical schools) either closer to home or more suited to their interests and/or academic abilities. Others became occasional students, taking terms off or, in a few cases, taking a course or two off campus. The university endeavors to keep its doors open so these students can return. Like most college students who discontinue their education, the black students who have dropped from college may intend eventually to finish. The few we were able to track down for interviews all denied they had terminated their education. It should be mentioned that, according to studies of project TALENT data, college attrition rates for blacks and whites are quite similar when students are matched in social class. (17)

The seniors we interviewed had experienced enough academic success to finish college. A majority of these students planned to continue education beyond undergraduate school, at least to a master's degree. In the latter case, especially for women, a frequent goal was a special area of education. Most black students at the University of Michigan (18) and in a multi-university and college sample felt their institution had contributed to their attempts to reach goals in life. At Michigan, our sample of black seniors were more satisfied with their academic experiences than were the white students sampled. In response to an open-ended question asking for their reactions to the university as an undergraduate institution, 63 percent of our black sample (vs. only 44 percent of the white sample) said the institution was at least good academically. The reasons given varied among students. Some said their education gave them the skills and knowledge needed to succeed in careers. Others said that college opened new areas, new insights. Still others, more often middle-class than working-class black students, said they felt college had given them experiences and skills needed to compete with whites in a white-controlled society, to "beat whitey at his own game." The major criticisms of the university as a set of academic experiences (much more frequent among whites than blacks) were that the courses or curricula were irrelevant or too academic, and the various requirements and evaluation methods were archaic and rigid. (20)

W. P. Fenstemacher factor analysed specially-admitted black students' questionnaire responses dealing with the experienced seriousness of 39 different potential problems of college students. The analysis yielded five problem areas: 1) academic pressures and resulting self-questioning; 2) lack of interest in courses, and a lack of self-discipline; 3) blame of the system, rather than self-blame for difficulties; 4) feeling lost or overwhelmed by and at the university; and 5) family problems. His data suggest the academic area as one of the most stressful, perhaps more than half of this sample (a mixed sample of freshmen, sophomores, juniors, and seniors) having experienced rather serious academic problems. Students tended to view their problems more as the product of poor high school preparation and stiff competition than as the result of their lacking the ability needed for college work.

He also notes that a large percentage of black students also experienced either a lack of interest in courses, or felt unable to buckle down and work as hard as necessary and in the ways necessary to succeed in their courses. His findings are consistent with our interviews of black seniors.

Fenstemacher points out the great reluctance of these students to seek remedial help at the university (for example, instruction in study skills and in the improvement of reading speed), which he suggests is the product of their experiences of marked academic success in high school and a resultant inability to acknowledge that they might need improvement in basic study skills. (21)

Our post-freshman year data suggested that blacks experienced a great deal of isolation and loneliness, especially the women. The retrospective reports of our interviewed black seniors reinforces this. However, by their senior year, most of these problems appear to have been resolved, at least for those students who stay on to complete their college work. Close friendships are established over time; boyfriends, girlfriends, lovers are found; prospective (or actual) husbands and wives are found in many cases.

The size and perceived personality of the institution itself is, for some students, even harder to cope with, and many students never do come to terms with it, except to counter it by drawing into a circle of friends. Fenstemacher's analysis sheds some light on the origins of these feelings of isolation and estrangement. He arrayed his sample of black students on the basis of their objectives for attending college along two dimensions. One indicated the strength of their instrumental objectives (i.e., the extent to which college, and success in courses, was viewed as a means to career and professional success). The second indicated the strength of their intellectual objectives (i.e., the extent to which their college study aimed at the development and pursuit of the subject matter of courses, independent of subsequent career payoff—except perhaps for the payoff accrued by the pursuit of a career in these academic fields). He found a slight tendency for the students with more instrumental orientations to be less isolated from other students. He also found a tendency (statistically not significant) for students with more intellectual orientations to find the university less awesome, more personal. (22)

If black students tend to have more instrumental orientations than other students (and a variety of data from several studies indicates this is the case), and if (perhaps increasingly) black students must depend on each other for friendships, sharing this orientation is part of the bond which facilitates friendships. On the other hand, if the faculty tends to encourage and support intellectual objectives of students, perhaps the more intellectual students find the faculty and classrooms friendlier, more personal and responsive to them.

It is also possible that the more intellectual students are better prepared for college work and are more successful in their courses. Thus they face less stress and frustration and are less likely to be faced with the task of hunting and finding personal help in dealing with their problems. These relationships are slight, however, and we should not make too much of them.

The size and impersonality of the university seems generally to present more of a problem to working-class than to non-working-class students, white or black. And, working-class whites have more instrumental orientations than do other whites. There is also some suggestion that working-class whites experience more social isolation than do other whites, at least in the arts and science curricula. Perhaps instrumentally-oriented students find a more congenial social atmosphere in the more instrumentally-oriented professional schools, such as engineering or nursing.

Fenstemacher's questionnaire data indicate that problems of loneliness are less serious than our interviews indicate. Perhaps the interview situation is better able to evoke personal problems, or can provide the time and mood to make the students' past more vivid. Or, perhaps, the dynamic of the interview situation can "create" problems where there are none. Or, perhaps, as more and more black students enter the university, and as the black student community becomes more cohesive and develops better internal contacts, the problems of loneliness diminish, especially the sense of personal isolation among other students. We looked only at the first sizable group of specially-admitted blacks. Fenstemacher looked as well at (and pooled) the experiences of the more numerous black students who followed.

To move away for a moment from the immediate question of

experiences, I want to describe something of black students' plans for their own futures. It has been often said that one of the primary results of a university education is that it moves large numbers of working-class students into the middle-class, by providing them access to middle-class jobs, and by providing them with appropriate styles of behavior, attitudes, and goals. Our interviews with black seniors indicate that a number, especially those from working-class origins, aspire to a more or less traditional middle-class life, comprising a happy marriage, children, a steady job, a nice house in a good neighborhood, and money for leisure and travel, perhaps coupled with a part-time or occasional (pre- and post-family) career for the wife. Again, this pattern seems most clear in the interviews with working-class black women. In some contrast, it appears that the white view of the good life, even for working-class students, is shifting somewhat away from this view, towards a future more oriented toward personal growth and expression, new and novel experiences, and some isolation from pressing and perhaps unsolvable social problems.

Again, to stretch the data a bit, it is almost as if blacks are being groomed to take over social roles and tasks which whites are leaving behind. Consistent with this is the tendency seen in our freshman data for blacks to evidence much more of the protestant work ethic than do whites. It is as if, in these respects at least, there is a generation gap between black and white students. As another example, many blacks find strange and stupid the preoccupation of many white students with drugs and the insides of their heads "while there are such serious problems outside in the world that need hard work."

We also looked at the extent to which black students planned to center their futures around helping the black community. For the most part, such plans were found among non-working-class black students, especially males (but the sample here was quite small and quite likely to be atypical even of the black and non-working-class black student group at Michigan). Several such students aimed at law or a position of power in business, and planned to move from such a position into politics or, more broadly, social action. Among working-class blacks, the orientation was toward more personal goals, suiting a job to their interests and skills, although often planning to do this job within the black community and thereby helping blacks. This appeared clearest, and a most congenial combination of self-fulfillment and help, among students planning to teach. (23)

The political activity of the increasingly cohesive black student community, especially the conflict with the university over the degree of effort the university makes in increasing the educational opportunity for black students, did seem to have a decided impact on the commitment of individual black students to the struggle of blacks for political and economic equality. A few black students who, when interviewed a year earlier as juniors, indicated that "being black" played a minor role in their conceptions of themselves and in their commitments to their people, responded differently in the senior interviews. Some said that the black-university conflict had made them aware, for the first time, of the indifference of white institutions to the problems and goals of the black people. A few indicated they were making a major reorientation of their work to make a more meaningful contribution to other blacks. (24)

Several studies (25) suggest that, across a variety of predoninantly white colleges and universities, most blacks (and a majority of whites) find college contributing positively to their personal goals and ambitions, and feel closer to the lives they want eventually to lead than before college. Most became more optimistic about their futures than before college. For some, a number of personal goals have been realized: making career decisions and learning to live with these decisions, finding potential husbands and wives, learning things about parts of the world that were inaccessible to them prior to college, gaining some self-confidence and a greater sense of competence in some hitherto questionable or unknown areas. Many feel their academic work has made a contribution to their futures. Some have gained information and skills which they feel are personally worthwhile and will contribute to achieving their own internalized goals through their careers. Others have obtained information and skills to overcome hurdles and meet challenges not of their own choosing. The latter view was most cynically put in one of our interviews: "I learned what Whitey thinks is important, his rules, so I can beat him at his own game."

For some blacks, college was, on the whole, a useful and pleasant experience. For others, college was useful, but not particularly enjoyable. For still others (only a minority of those we interviewed at the University of Michigan) college was neither useful nor enjoyable. For this last group, college meant a variety of things: an estrangement from their own black community, their families and friends; a learning of things which seemed useless and artificial, too abstract and intellectual; a series of unpleasant experiences with faculty and other students; having personal problems which they couldn't solve and which they could not get competent help to solve.

With respect to this last, the reader is reminded of Fenstemacher's comments about the reluctance of black students to seek remedial help. This reluctance seems to extend to psychological counselling as well. One counselor who has worked extensively with black students at a college reports how slowly and reluctantly black students came to her for help; first one, then a few, then finally a number. Some simply needed assurance that the academic and personal problems they were facing were not peculiarly theirs, or theirs because they were black, but were problems faced by many, if not most, students at some time or other. Perhaps this reluctance would be diminished if schools hired competent black counselors, who worked not only in individual and small group counseling situations, but who also had other and frequent informal contacts with individual black students and black groups in other settings. Acknowledging that one has a personal problem which he needs help to solve, and then going to the semi-institutional place where such help is available and signing on as a client (perhaps being placed on a waiting list) is hard for any person, perhaps especially for a student to whom so much of the university environment is strange and frustrating.

Some Special Nuances: Questions, Hypotheses, But Little Data

Black Students at Black Colleges

Little, if any, systematic research has been done on the experiences of black students at predominantly black colleges. We do know that there are systematic differences in temperament, attitudes, and goals between black students who enter predominantly black colleges and those who enter white schools. The latter, generally speaking, are more independent, liberal, more concerned with social justice, less vocational in their purposes in attending college, and more likely to have plans to attend graduate school. Those who attend black schools report more parental pressure to attend college. Black students attending white institutions evidence greater pre-college achievement, by and large, than their counterparts attending black schools. (26)

In an all-black environment, one would expect the pressures and stresses students face to be somewhat different. The experience of being lonely and isolated in a hostile or indifferent environment should be far less prevalent than in a large, predominantly white, university. Academic stresses should be less, since institutions tend to set academic standards to meet the competence of their students. Do academically competent black students feel more competent and satisfied at a black school where the competition is less severe, or at a white institution where the competition is keener? We cannot answer this question at present. Some evidence suggests that, given any level of pre-college-measured achievement, students learn as much at black as white institutions—at least as measured by standardized tests like the GRE. (27)

Blacks attending small, white, liberal arts colleges, may have experiences somewhere in between. Certainly size is not a source of stress as it is in a large, white university. However, these liberal arts colleges are white. Whether they are more personal, more concerned, more tolerant, more responsive to the needs of black students, may vary widely from college to college.

*The Visibility
of the Specially-Admitted Black Student*

Many, if not most, colleges and universities have black students who were admitted via regular admissions procedures. When a college announces, amid fanfare, a "special opportunity admissions program," some faculty, administrators, and students suddenly "discover" that there are black students on the campus and in their classes. They may, unfortunately, come to perceive any black student they contact as specially-admitted and for that reason not quite up to the demands of college work. One faculty member admitted to being very suspicious of the good work turned in by one black student, only to discover to his chagrin that the student "really is smart and not specially-admitted at all." It is sad, and hurts the student, that these suspicions are aroused and that evidence of "regular" admission is sufficient to clear the suspicion.

Of course, black students sense this and experience it often. One black student's remarks may be paraphrased as follows, "I was having academic difficulty and went in to see an academic counselor. I told him my problem, and his reaction was, in effect: 'Of course you are having trouble, specially-admitted students will have trouble here.'"

The Critical Mass

In a large, predominantly white school, perhaps even in a small school, black students may have very different experiences depending on whether there are 15, or 150, or 1500 black students on the campus, and whether there is, near the campus, a large and varied black community. When the black student population is tiny, the isolation may be crushing, especially where black-white relationships are damaged by wariness, mistrust, and hostility. When large, there can be black cohesion, group activities, more opportunities for congenial and close relationships, communal space, etc. When extremely large, the black student community may fragment, even war, on ideological issues. When (as in a few urban universities) the institution is vast, the black population is quite large and there is a large black community nearby from which students commute, the students may again experience isolation, anonymity, loneliness, and an indifferent or even a hostile environment at the institution. Again, this has not been studied relative to the black student experience, although some of these factors have been studied with respect to the experiences of white students at different kinds and sizes of schools.

The Black Graduate Students

Systematic research on the black graduate students, especially those admitted via special recruiting programs, has not yet been reported. Compared with undergraduate studies, graduate studies demand more intense academic commitments, and make stronger professional role demands on students. They demand more independence, more inner-direction, and more resourcefulness (at least in some senses). They can provide more personal attention and more flexibility than can often be provided in undergraduate programs. How do these students fare?

Awareness "of my Blackness"

One of the toughest and most ambiguous issues confronting black students concerns how they want their blackness acknowledged. There appears to be, within the black student community and probably within individual black students, a profound ambivalence on this issue, an ambivalence that permeates encounters with white students, as well as reactions to black studies, black-institution negotiations, remedial programs, etc. Although this may be superficial, perhaps the feelings of many black students can be summarized as follows:

I want to be responded to as a full and unique human being. Part of my being is being black, which means that my heritage is not white and western European, yet to me it is important, and very real. You can make academic demands on me, but I can make demands that you change your institution to better serve blacks. I don't like to acknowledge the possibility that I need remedial help, but I do—not because I am black, but because I have not been well taught. Teach me the facts and skills I need to do what I want to do, but do not try to force your manners or style or values on me. If I want them I will take them, but it is my choice.

Recommendations for Colleges and Universities

1) Colleges and universities should plan special admissions programs for black students which are consonant with the particular resources and goals of the institution, and with those of the students they mean to bring in. They must set up such programs with the full awareness and support of their faculties, and these faculties must keep aware and informed of the programs.

2) If a college's black community wishes to run remedial programs for black students, they should be fully supported and encouraged; the programs should be carefully evaluated, constantly monitored and improved. If the institution wishes to undertake a remedial program, it should be color-blind. All programs should be tailored to the individual student. Ideally, such remedial programs should be easily accessible to the students and operate in close contact with the students' classroom instructors.

3) Students, black or white, should be treated as unique, whole individuals. Their work should be evaluated, their problems dealt

with, their promise judged, as the product of an individual, not as the product of a "black" or "specially-admitted" student. The student, the instructor (or counselor), and the instruction (or counseling) process get corrupted when this is not done, whether the student is prejudged as defective, or carried along in the belief "he will catch hold later."

4) Counseling and advising programs should be humanized and better informed, and put in closer touch with the teaching faculty so that the student is adequately treated, and so that those who work with him do not work at cross-purposes. I know of one instance where a faculty member, believing that his struggling black students would complete his course quite successfully—every student struggled early in the course—constantly encouraged them to stick to the course only to find later, to his amazement, that the students' academic counselor had strongly and successfully encouraged them to drop the course. Ideally, teaching faculty should work in concert on the academic problems of students they share.

5) Student services, and facilities for student activities should be easily and readily available at no cost to all campus groups, formal and informal, large and small. There should be spacious, informal, private places for dances, parties, or just get-togethers.

6) Special admissions programs should be thoroughly and constantly evaluated, by persons outside the program. Weaknesses and strengths should be constantly assessed. The causes of individual student failure and breakdown should be carefully determined, and the results fed back into the program development process.

7) It is difficult to recommend ways to cope with the wariness and mistrust so often reported in black-white student relationships. Many suggestions have been made over time. One is to put blacks and whites together in settings so each can learn how he comes across to others. Another is for the institution to move quickly and decisively to eliminate sources of needless and thoughtless racial friction. But these again are platitudes and only scratch the surface. The sources of wariness and mistrust are manifold, including white prejudice and guilt, black fear and insecurity. They are contaminated by artificial and external factors, such as the demand by some militant blacks to politicize certain aspects of interpersonal relationships. (28) We will probably have to live with this climate for some time. And the climate will vary dramatically from campus to campus, depending in large part on the mix of students, the racial issues which surface, and how they are handled.

Notes

(1) W. P. Fenstemacher, *A Study of the Relationship of Instrumental and Intellectual Orientations to the Educational Experiences of Black Students at the University of Michigan.* Final Report to USOE, Grant # OEG-5-9-325072-0047 [010], (Ann Arbor: University of Michigan, 1971); J. M. Hedegard, and D. R. Brown, "Encounters of Some Negro and White Freshmen With a Public Multiversity," *Journal of Social Issues* 25 (1969): 131-144; and J. M. Hedegard, *Longitudinal Study of Working-Class College Students.* Final Report to USOE, Grant # OEG-5-70-0010 [010], (Ann Arbor: University of Michigan, 1971).

(2) J. A. Centra, "Black Students at Predominantly White Colleges: A Research Description." *Sociology of Education* 43 (1970): 325-339; and R. T. Hartnett, "Differences in Selected Attitudes and College Orientations Between Black Students Attending Traditionally Negro and Traditionally White Institutions," *Sociology of Education* 43 (1970): 419-436.

(3) J. K. Folger, H. S. Astin, and A. E. Bayer. *Human Resources in Higher Education* (New York: Russell Sage, 1970).

(4) K. A. Feldman and T. M. Newcomb, *The Impact of College on Students.* Vol. I (San Francisco: Jossey-Bass, 1969).

(5) Hedegard and Brown, *op. cit.*

(6) Fenstemacher, *op cit.;* Hedegard, *op. cit.*

(7) Centra, *op. cit.*

(8) Hedegard and Brown, *op. cit.*

(9) *Ibid.*

(10) *Ibid.;* Hedegard, *op. cit.*

(11) Hedegard and Brown, *ibid.*

(12) Hedegard, *op. cit.*

(13) *Ibid.*

(14) Fenstemacher, *op. cit.*

(15) Hedegard, *op. cit.*

(16) J. A. Centra, R. L. Linn, and M. E. Parry, "Academic Growth in Predominantly Negro and White Colleges," *American Educational Research Journal* 7 (1970): 83-98.

(17) Folger, *et al., op. cit.*

(18) Hedegard, *op. cit.*

(19) Centra, *op. cit.*

(20) Hedegard, *op. cit.*

(21) Fenstemacher, *op. cit.*

(22) *Ibid.*

(23) Hedegard, *op. cit.*

(24) *Ibid.*

(25) Centra, *op. cit.;* Fenstemacher, *op. cit.;* Hedegard, *ibid.*

(26) Hartnett, *op. cit.*

(27) Centra, *et al., op. cit.*

(28) C. Donald, Jr., "Cornell: A Confrontation in Black and White," in C. Strout and D. J. Grossvogel (eds.), *Divided We Stand: Reflections on the Crisis at Cornell* (Garden City: Doubleday-Anchor, 1971).

IV

The Black Community and Black Students in White Colleges and Universities

Edward J. Barnes

Introduction

Of all the institutions of the society whose legitimacy has been called into question, perhaps none has felt the effects of this scrutiny as keenly as the American system of education. The challenge issues from diverse quarters, the major charges being that 1) it has failed to provide education commensurate with the needs of a rapidly changing society and world and 2) that it has virtually ignored the existence and needs of the society's oppressed low-status minority groups: blacks, chicanos, original Americans, and Puerto Ricans. The Report of the National Advisory Commission on Civil Disorders, popularly known as the Kerner Report, asserts:

Education in a democratic society must equip the children of the nation to realize their potential and to participate fully in American life. . . . But for many minorities and paticularly the children of the racial ghetto, the school has failed to provide the educational experience which could help to overcome the effects of discrimination and deprivation. This failure is one of the persistent sources of grievance and resentment within the Negro community. The hostility of black parents and students toward the school system is generating increasing conflict and causing disruptions within many school districts. (1)

Though this observation by the Kerner Commission refers directly to the pre-college sector of the American education system, it has indirect implications for post-secondary education as it relates to the admission question. Historically, admission into white colleges and universities has been based on narrowly defined admission requirements. Minority students, particularly black students, typically have been judged as unqualified on the basis of these admission criteria. Even those students who could meet the academic and entrance examination requirements were generally eliminated by prohibitive tuition and other costs of attending the institution. Thus, the majority of black students, desiring to attend a college or university, but unable to meet the expenses and/or the admission requirements of the white institution, went to less prestigious schools, often located far from home and in the South.

Prior to the Kerner Commission Report, others (2) had pointed up the inequities existing in the educational arena as well as their consequences for the "victims" and for the society. The general civil inequality of black Americans was also pointed up by the marches of Dr. Martin Luther King, Jr. and the Southern Christian Leadership Conference in the late 1950's, and by the sit-in protests by black college students in the early and mid 1960's. But these reports or activities did not make much impact until the eruption of major violence in the urban centers of Watts, Detroit, Newark, and Cleveland in the mid through late 1960's and until the wave of disruptions following the assassination of Dr. Martin Luther King, Jr. Following these events and in response to intense pressure from black students and the black community, white colleges and universities throughout the country implemented hastily developed programs geared to bring about greater responsiveness to the national black community's needs and demands. The response in terms of black student enrollment is indicated by the fact that at the undergraduate level in 1965, of a total enrollment of 4.5 million students, it is estimated that blacks constituted about 4.5 percent or 207,316. By 1967 this figure had risen to 245,410, or to 5.15 percent of 4,764,834 students. By 1971 the enrollments of blacks had increased to represent 6 percent of the nation's college enrollment. (3) More importantly, until the decade of the 1960's traditional black colleges, which represent four percent of the 2,300 American undergraduate institutions, accounted for the bulk of black student enrollments. But, by 1971, traditionally white institutions were enrolling 53 percent of black college undergraduates in the nation. However, it should be noted that the average estimate of the proportion of black students at any given white college or university is small, about two percent. (4)

Nevertheless, this shift in enrollment patterns on the part of blacks in these institutions brings one face to face with some critical issues:

1) What are some implications for the black student as student and as member of the black community?
2) What are some implications for the black community as it impacts the black student?

3) What are some implications for the relationship between the black student and his community?

In addressing these issues we should be ever mindful of the context in which the increase in numbers of black students in white institutions originally occurred and continues to occur. Some of the distinguishing characteristics of that context are: the emergence of black consciousness as a salient phenomenon of the times, the great push toward group unity on the part of American blacks, diverse and conflicting notions regarding goals, strategies, and tactics in the black struggle, and the separation of the student from his reference group.

This discussion examines some of the relations between the black community and the black student in a white college or university. This analysis will be done within the framework of the concept "black consciousness." "Black consciousness" can be viewed as an ideological construct referring to an attitudinal-behavioral complex which includes as one of its components an emphasis on self-definition, self-determination, and activism on the part of blacks. This conception is based on a recognition of and respect for one's heritage, and on a positive valuation of action perceived as beneficial for black people as a collective.

The Black Community— Nature and Structure

Any analysis which involves the "black community," conceived as a collective entity, readily lends itself to glib generalizations and oversimplifications. If this pitfall is to be avoided, American blacks as a group must be viewed as highly complex, heterogeneous, and diverse. Even though, in this society, black people are viewed as a group apart from other people, and as showing common intragroup attributes, behaviors, and conditions, great variations are also obvious. (5) A. Billingsley offers the concept "ethnic subsociety as a means of capturing this duality. (6) An ethnic group is a relatively large configuration of people with a "shared feeling of peoplehood." In this society such groups are organized around race, religion, national origin, or some combination of these. M. Gordon states that common to the ethnic group

is the social-psychological element of a special sense of both ancestral and future-oriented identification with the group. These are the 'people' of my ancestors; therefore they are my people, and will be the people of my children and their children. With members of other groups I may share political participation, occupational relationships, common civic enterprise, perhaps even an occasional warm friendship. But in a very special way, which history has decreed, I share a sense of indissoluble and intimate identity with *this group* and *not that one* within the larger society and the world. (7)

This conception seems to reflect the reality of black Americans. As members of a color caste system, (8) and by virtue of our common peoplehood, black people are one, yet we do not form a homogeneous mass. In this vein, St. Clair Drake states that all American blacks are subject to victimization at the hands of the American social system. (9) In other words, all American blacks are relegated to a caste system and, as such, play subordinate roles in the society. But the caste system is itself structured into class levels. Billingsley makes use of three dimensions in describing the black community as an ethnic subsociety: social class, rural or urban residence, and region of country lived in. (10) For our purposes then, black people are not only blacks to be compared with whites; they may also be upper-class, middle-class, or lower-class, with northern, southern, or western residence, with rural or urban backgrounds, and significantly they may be meaningfully compared with each other.

As indicated by both Billingsley and St. Clair Drake (11) the caste-class analysis provides a useful frame of reference for studying the behavior of individuals and groups located at various positions in the social structure. Further, analyses from this frame of reference take into consideration the different types of identities people share. Gordon conceptualizes these identities as "historical" and "participational." The ethnic group is the locus of a sense of historical identification. The intersection of ethnicity and social class is the locus of participational identification.

With a person of the same social class but of a different ethnic group, one shares behavioral similarities but not a sense of peoplehood. With those of the same ethnic group but different social class, one shares the sense of peoplehood but not behavioral similarities. The only group which meets both of these criteria are people of the same ethnic group *and* same social class. (12)

As Billingsley suggests, (13) even though social class lines among American blacks are less rigid than among other groups of the society, social class distinctions within the black community do provide a distinct basis of differentiation which helps to condition the lives of its members.

Thus, when one speaks of the American black community as it relates to the American black student in the white college or university he has to be mindful of the complexity of the situation of which he speaks. The following discussion of the black student in the white institution is organized around this conception of the national black community.

The Black College Student— Past and Present

In the past, the presence of the black student in the white institution was not independent of his locus and that of his family in the class structure of the black community. Black students who served as integrators of white colleges came mainly from the middle and upper class strata of the black community. They were the children of Frazier's "black burgeoisie." While ethnically their identification was with the black community, their participational identification (behavior, style, preferences) approximated that of their white counterpart. They were "well read," "well dressed," and "well behaved," as viewed by the norms prevailing in the institutional situation. At a time when colleges stressed elitism and exclusiveness, these characteristics make the black student more acceptable to white students, teachers, and administrators. However this state of affairs was destructive to the black student's ethnic identity, in that his experiences within that setting worked toward alienating him from his community. He was expected to be a passive recipient of "information" and "knowledge" dispensed by the professors. Whatever they said had to be listened to without protest no matter how questionable, invalid, or humiliating. Those in charge of the situation appeared to operate from the premise that the black is an immature white and to become a whole mature person he had to be made white. The greater the transformation along these lines, the greater his acceptability to the white institution.

In response to the pressures generated by Civil Rights activities of the late 1950's, student protests of the early and mid 1960's and the uprisings in the black communities in the mid and late 1960's, white colleges and universities began to broaden the population of students to include students from lower class sectors of the black community. These students are generally referred to by such appellations as the "culturally deprived" or the "disadvantaged." This student represented an "alien" within the walls of academe. He brought new styles, orientations, etc. At the same time the more middle-class student, previously known in that setting, was bringing to the institution a new outlook and posture. He no longer felt constrained to be passive and receptive, but was beginning to question and challenge where before he had been accepting and compliant. In a word, the colleges and universities found themselves hosting a new breed of black students.

As it became increasingly obvious that psychology, sociology, and literature defined blacks as pathological and as social problems, it was also becoming increasingly obvious that the white society had little commitment to modifying the victimized status of blacks. Concurrently, black students were most keenly attuned to the facts of white racism and inequality; they were seeking a frame for viewing members of their community as normal rather than pathological. The revolutions in Africa served to quicken their interests in the improvement of the condition of blacks in America. Paralleling the progressive rise of "black consciousness" in the national black community, and in some sense serving as an impetus for it, black students banding together in black student unions challenged colleges and universities to become relevant to the needs of the black community. They stated clearly their refusals to suffer alienation from this community, its history, and its culture, regardless of their locus in its class structure.

Emergence of Black Consciousness— Some Areas of Conflict

The positive effects of black awareness cannot be denied. Some of these effects or correlates are: 1) increased awareness of and insight into the social system, 2) greater insight into the conditions, past and present, of blacks in this society, 3) the refusal to continue accepting blame for the group's victimized status, 4) increased awareness of, and the repudiation of, assimilation as a goal for blacks, 5) increased self and group esteem, and 6) increased unity among all segments of the black ethnic subsociety.

In fact black students, as a subset of the larger black community, were and are able to challenge successfully the white institutions of higher education primarily because of their relatedness to the larger black community. In his former capacity as faculty advisor to a black student organization, the writer frequently heard students assert that their "real" power lay in the local black community. This realization was reflected in activities on the part of the students to diminish the barriers between the university and the local black community. For example, the black student organization numbered among its membership nonstudent members of the local black community. Finally, when student protesters took over the university computer center, they received a great deal of support from that local community.

However, the changes attendant upon the emergence of black consciousness are not without their conflictive aspects. This should not come as a surprise since all growth or change involves conflict for those involved. In the national black community this is clearly indicated by the diversity of opinions, beliefs, and predilections, characterizing various segments of that community, with respect to what the goals of black people should be, what strategies and tactics should be utilized. Indeed such ideological differences often prevent a consensus regarding the differentiation among objectives, strageties, and tactics respectively. Some observers of the current scene perceive a relationship between the ideological position with respect to these factors and one's position in the social structure. Those having the least at stake are more prone to choose the most radical objectives (revolution rather than reform, separation rather than full participation, etc.). (14) Conflict is also reflected in the confusion around symbols and substance of blackness, for example, style of dress, linguistic usages, and hair styles.

These conflicting trends, in the black community, are also reflected in the black student populations of white college campuses, particularly now that these bodies have representation from throughout the black subsociety.

Now differences of opinion, per se, need not be negative in effect. The significance of such differences turns on the meanings attributed to them. Frequently students tend to attribute negative import to views deviant from those they hold. This tendency is particularly prominent among those students designating themselves as revolutionaries. They are likely to refer to others who do not fully subscribe to their living styles, ideologies, etc., by such epithets as "Uncle Toms," "House Niggers," "Oreos" (from the Oreo cookie—a chocolate cookie with white filling), etc. This kind of judgmental behavior clearly is divisive in effect, giving rise to the "blacker than thou" syndrome, whereby pernicious grading practices were carried out. One major outcome of this practice is the tendency to bestow the grade of "authentic black" only upon the poor, inner city inhabitant. Apparently this tendency toward "ideological imposition" is based, in part, on the failure to comprehend the complex nature of the black ethnic subsociety. Because of the emphasis on cohesiveness, many blacks, students and university staff, behave as though heterogeneity does not exist among blacks.

The effects of ideological imposition can also be seen in the problems many black students have in developing and implementing task-oriented activities of potential benefit to blacks. A great deal of time and energy is spent in endless "rapping" in an attempt to have a given ideological position embraced by all. In these instances talk seemingly becomes a substitute for action. The writer has experienced the ironic situation in which the attempt at organizing around a program of activity ended in a fruitless discussion which attempted to fit the concept of "functional unity" into a given ideological framework.

Depending upon the ideological predilection of staff and students, pressures are likely to be applied in the recruiting/selection process or in the counseling/scheduling process with the intention of having students pursue those areas where the black experience can provide an immediate and obvious input (social science or black studies). With respect to course scheduling, the problems stemming from demands for obvious and immediate relevance derive, in part, from this source. The problem is that course material not perceived as having these attributes is given to blanket indictment, where such indictment properly should be made against the traditional behaviors of practitioners in those disciplines. For example, many black students in the social sciences charge that the techniques of research are irrelevant. This judgment is based on the nature of the research traditionally done by whites in the black community. Rejection occurs because of the victimization of the black community by white researchers and because much of this research is perceived, and rightly so, as being invalid and harmful to the black community. But the critical factor is that instead of criticizing certain researchers such as A. F. Jensen's or D. P. Moynihan's conclusions and inferences, there is rejection of the entire research endeavor.

Now probably most of those who adopt this position would readily agree that the liberation of blacks involves the need to reconstruct the experience of blacks in an accurate way, that it involves the necessity to reformulate white explanations of black life and thought, and that it also involves an acute need for authentic and sensitive research into many aspects of the black experience. If this is the case, then obviously blacks must possess the necessary research skills and competencies to carry out these aims. Obviously this position is incompatible with rejection of the research endeavor.

Given the dearth of knowledge and information about the physical sciences and mathematics in the black community, they are often seen as tangential or irrelevant in the struggle for black liberation, even by students within the university. Black students who do bring a firm background in these areas are frequently reluctant to pursue them, given their perceived lack of relevance to the black struggle by many blacks. The net effects are that the black community loses since, whether the ultimate objective is full participation in the current society or separatism, skills in these areas are imperative in the struggle for self-determination. Probably the most destructive aspect of this state of affairs is that it can be easily turned into a device for deception. That is, many black students who fear they may not be able to perform competently in the various disciplines are sanctioned in their indictment and subsequent dismissal of them as "irrelevant."

The black student from the lower socioeconomic inner city family, the relative newcomer to the white campus, has special difficulties to cope with in addition to those created by the disjunction of his earlier educational experience and that required or expected by the institution. This is particularly the case for the black student attending an urban college in or near his home community. Given the focus on contributing to the community and on relevance in the black struggle, many students are torn between being in college and making a commitment to the pursuit of academic objectives and remaining in the community. The problem seems to revolve around the separation of his membership group from his reference group. In the instance where the reference group continues to be peers in the home community who did not go on to college, the student experiences his severest conflict. The actions of black students have resulted in the college or university campus being more open to the black community than ever before. One outcome is that the number of young adults, from the immediate community, to be found on campus at any given time (day or night) is fairly large. Often they exert a strong pull on the student and compete with his academic pursuits and demands for his time. In many cases the student does not desire to participate in the activities of these youth (pool shooting, movies, riding around, parties, etc.) but feels constrained to do so lest his behavior be interpreted as "going middle-class" or "getting too good for his friends". The extent to which this situation can pose a severe problem for the student is shown in the following case:

John N. entered the university through a special program. He was born, reared, and attended public school in the community in which the university is located. He is from an intact family, and is the oldest male of a sibship of three girls and two boys. His father was employed as a laborer in a steel mill and his mother was employed as a laundry worker. The family lives in one of the most economically depressed sections of the local black community. John and his sibs attended the high school in his area. The proportion of graduates who go on to college is the lowest of any school in the community. He graduated in the third fifth of his high school class and scored less than 900 on the Scholastic Aptitude Test (SAT). Nevertheless he was a serious, hardworking young man. One day he sought out the writer, asking about the possibility of transfer to an institution out of the state. Exploration of his motivations revealed that four of his high school and neighborhood friends were with him practically 24 hours a day. They were staying in his dormitory room, "bumming" meal tickets (often the student's) for use in the student cafeteria. He was never able to study in his room because of noise, music, and other distractions, and would be chided by them when he went to the library. They were constantly after him to join them at the pool table or go on jaunts which would keep them up most of the night. The final outcome which brought him to the writer was that he was failing each of his courses. He felt the only way he could salvage his situation was by leaving the city. He was not able to resist the demands of his friends and expressed feeling guilty about having something they did not have, and about not being "out in the community doing something" for his people. The writer moved this student into a room with a student from out of state, and personally counselled him over a period of two months during which time the student's conflicts around his relationship to his family and his friends were explored and handled. Clearly, situations of this sort constitute barriers to student performance.

The situation for the commuter student from the economically depressed home is similar. Often the parents have little or no concept of what college attendance means in terms of demands on and expectations held toward the student. This means that the style which prevailed in the household when the student was in public school is maintained after his admission to college. Activities such as reading a book, making notes, sitting in reflection, etc., are not perceived as active involvement. Rather, under these conditions the student is seen as available for verbal interaction, running errands, baby sitting, etc.

In addition, living quarters are usually crowded, space being at a premium, and since generally a good deal of the time of family members is spent watching television and playing records, there is no place of quiet and privacy for studying. Youngsters often feel guilty about leaving home to live in dormitories and when they do, often spend every free moment at home, with the result that studies are neglected. Here, too, a barrier to performance is erected.

On the basis of the foregoing it appears that various interactions between the student and the community can have either a facilitating or an inhibiting effect on the black student in the white college. However it appears that inhibiting effects need not be inevitable. The student can identify with his ethnic group and at the same time engage in those behaviors (participational identification) which are necessary to move successfully through the institution. This means, among other things, behaving in accord with the demand characteristics of the learning situation, a fact which does not necessarily carry the implication of assimilating the values of the institution which are contrary to those of one's ethnic group. To deny this means to deny the possibility of independence between one's philosophies and his training. For example, the competent and successful black engineer will behave in a fashion similar to the competent white engineer with respect to matters of engineering, but this does not mean, *ipso facto,* that the black engineer will be without a sense of identification with the black community. This points up the import of maintaining a distinction between ethnic identification, on the one hand, and participational identification, on the other. Or to put it another way, for our purposes it is crucial that we distinguish between those behaviors dictated by roles from those behaviors coming from the personality (values, beliefs, attitudes, etc.). The ability to distinguish between oneself and the role one plays is a critical operation for blacks. A succinct statement of the role-person distinction is reflected in the old black folk song: "got one mind for white folks to see, 'nother for what I know is me. . . ." (15)

Another manner in which the black student's interaction with his community has a determining influence upon his experience in the white college setting concerns what he has been led to believe about himself up to that point. In many urban high schools, inappropriate behaviors of black students are legitimated and reinforced. Since "black consciousness" is frequently equated with "militance" on the part of student or parent, or both, some teachers are intimidated and feel pressured to evaluate academic performance more favorably than the facts of the matter warrant. As a result, many black students enter the university with unrealistic notions of the energy and efforts they must expend for a given payoff. Secondly, a policy of social promotion, as practiced in many school systems, creates the illusion of progress and provides the student with erroneous feedback about his level of performance. Some of the more "liberal" instructors show a tendency to compensate for the students' oppressed condition, past and present, in their evaluation of them. All of these practices result in the student arriving on the college scene with a distorted academic self-concept. A student previously defined as a good student will more than likely continue to behave in those ways productive of that evaluation after he enters the college or university. Consequently, those who have not been accurately assessed are almost certain to encounter difficulty in the physical sciences, mathematics, and the quantitatively oriented social sciences. This is the point at which "black awareness" is likely to contribute to the problem. Since one of the outcomes of the black movement has been to throw into sharp relief the operations and practices of the racist American social system, black students can invoke "white racism" for failure and maintain cognitive consistency with the black ideology ("the course is irrelevant," "the professor is racist," etc.). When this position is adopted as a coping mechanism, tutoring and/or counselling efforts, undertaken by the institution or by special intervention programs, are almost doomed to ineffectiveness. When the black university staff (counselors and instructors) sanction the student in this approach, he is almost destined to later failure and drop out. Even when they are aware that the student has invoked "white racism" as a rationalization of his own failure, whatever its source, many black staff find it difficult not to sanction the student in this maneuver either by omission or commission. This reluctance is frequently related to the fear of being perceived as "whiter than whitey."

Conflict With Environment

The emergence of black consciousness in and the struggle for liberation by the black community has had another indirect effect on the black student as he functions in the white academic community. As noted previously, the number of black students in white universities has increased greatly in the past few years. In addition a large proportion now come from lower socioeconomic families or situations. Various studies (16) and subjective observations indicate that children from lower-class families tend to be raised to adhere to external proscriptions and behavior within highly structured environments. Thus, we frequently find these black students in need of a clearly structured situation, one in which the demand characteristics are clearly articulated. At the same time, the university is becoming progressively less structured to meet the demands of middle- and upper-class white students. This situation takes on added gravity when related to the relationship between structured and the student's perception of the availability of and use of resources. In a loosely structured situation, the black inner city student not only does not utilize extant resources, he does not even perceive their existence. An often heard comment in this regard is "no one told me about it." It appears that if he is to make use of available resources, the situation must be structured to facilitate such utilization.

With a decrease in structure there is a corresponding decrease in the number of formal feedback opportunities (tests, homework recitation, etc.). Considering this in relation to the issue raised earlier regarding perceptions of academic efficiency, it is obvious that it becomes increasingly difficult for the student to recognize the gap between expectations and performance. In this respect, in the writer's experience, it is commonplace for the "special admit" black student to misjudge his grade in a given course by two to three letter grades. A lack of structure often contributes to this and to the student's misjudgment of the pace of a given course which, in turn, affects course performance, since it usually results in the student being overwhelmed with work towards the end of the academic term.

The structure variable also interacts with the time orientation variable. According to several writers (17), lower socioeconomic groups differ from middle- and upper-class groups in time orientation (present vs. future). If this is the case, then the lower-status black student in a loosely structured situation may not receive the message that he will be held responsible for what occurs in class regardless of whether he is present or absent. This hypothesis seems to be supported by the fact that the students frequently voice disturbance over not having been required to attend class, turn in homework, and make up work missed when they receive low evaluations at the end of the term.

A further implication of loose structure with respect to these students concerns the mode of approach to tasks. There is a general tendency to assume a working strategy which emphasizes a time-period factor rather than the task itself. For example, a 9-5, Monday through Friday, working strategy is frequently adopted as compared to a strategy which stresses working until the task is complete. It is critical that the black community both inside and outside the university recognize those strategies and orientations likely to facilitate the student's successful movement through the system, and interact with him in a manner to insure that he makes maximum use of those educational experiences available to him. This assertion is based on the assumption that the greatest need of the black community is for the full range of skills and competencies required to cope with and get on in a rapidly changing, complex, urban society. In what he referred to as "education for black power" Dr. Matthew Holden states:

. . . The new mission will be to avoid the speciousness of developing students into mere verbalists, sophists, and rhetoricians. If there is a single obvious difficulty with current students . . . it is their addiction to a language of social action without an honest and sustained attention to the facts underlying that reality or the logic involved in any proposal to change that reality. If mature black intellectuals have failed in any significant way, it is that they have become intimidated by student militancy. . . . (18)

In suggesting a strategy for education for the implementation of black power, Dr. Holden states:

The business of the black intellectual, in forwarding the development of other intellectuals (his students) is to tell the truth (or as much as he can discover) and to aid in imaginative searches for ways to make the truthful situation most productive. This is what we mean and what we must insist upon—in "the regimen of fact and logic."

This is a vital part of our understanding of liberal education—the education appropriate to a man who will be a man of power. To be a man of power means that one must acquire a strategic position such that one can survive, grow, and develop—even in adverse circumstances.

. . . the objective in black education, is therefore, to provide those forms of training which will most greatly enhance the black man's capacities to penetrate the strategic points of influence and decision. (19)

The position proffered by Dr. Holden, the writer believes, is consistent with the notion that the black community must, through its various subsets, apprehend the facilitating features ensuing from emerging black consciousness and black identification, while working to diminish the negative aspects and utilize them in the educational process. This is particularly relevant for the black student in the white academic setting, for it is here that the greatest potential for conflict, intrapersonal and intragroup, exists. The black community cannot afford to allow the conflicts generated in the process of the black struggle and exacerbated by white academics to deny it the skills and resources needed to get it from where it is to where it has to go.

Notes

(1) *Report of the National Advisory Commission on Civil Disorders* (Washington, D. C.: United States Government Printing Office, 1968), pp. 424-425.
(2) K. B. Clark, "The Negro College Student: Some Facts and Some Concerns," *Journal of the Association of College Admission Counselors* 9 (1964): 11-14; H. M. Bond, *Education of the Negro in the American Social Order* (New York: Prentice-Hall, 1934).
(3) Southern Regional Education Board News Release, October, 1971, Atlanta, Georgia; Gordon D. Morgan, *The Ghetto College Student: A Descriptive Essay on College Youth from the Inner City* (Iowa City, Iowa: The American College Testing Program, Inc., 1970), p. 15.
(4) A. E. Bayer, and R. F. Boruch, *The Black Student in American Colleges* (Washington, D. C.: American Council on Education, 1969), p. 1; Gordon D. Morgan, *op. cit.,* p. 15.
(5) See St. Clair Drake, "The Social and Economic Status of the Negro in the United States," in E. Foner, ed., *America's Black Past* (New York: Harper and Row, 1970), pp. 501-520, for a treatment of the class structure of the black subsociety and the caste-class conception.
(6) A. Billingsley, *Black Families in White America* (Englewood Cliffs, N. J.: Prentice-Hall, 1968).
(7) M. Gordon, *Assimilation in American Life* (New York: Oxford University Press, 1964), p. 29.
(8) Drake, *op. cit.* p. 503.
(9) *Ibid.*
(10) Billingsley, *op. cit.*

(11) *Ibid.*, and Drake, *op. cit.*
(12) Gordon, *op. cit.* p. 53.
(13) Billingsley, *op. cit.*
(14) Drake, *op. cit.*
(15) R. Ames, "Protest and Irony in Negro Folksong," *Social Science* 14 (1950): 193-213.
(16) T. Adorno, *et al., The Authoritarian Personality* (New York: Harper & Row, 1950); M. Kohn, "Social Class and the Exercise of Parental Authority," *American Sociological Review*, 24 (1959): 352-366; R. D. Hess, and Virginia C. Shipman, "Early Experience and the Socialization of Cognitive Modes in Children," *Child Development* 36 (1965): 169-186; S. Lipset, "American Student Activism," in G. Weaver and J. Weaver, eds., *The University and Revolution* (Englewood Cliffs, N. J.: Prentice-Hall, 1969).
(17) W. Mischel, "Theory and Research on the Antecedents of Self-Imposed Delay of Reward," in B. Maher, ed., *Progress in Experimental Personality Research,* Vol. 3, (New York: Academic Press, 1966); N. Johnson, and P. Sanday, "Cultural Variations in an Urban Poor Population," Carnegie Mellon Action Project, Research Report #1, (Pittsburgh: Carnegie Mellon University, 1969), (mimeographed); B. Rosen, "Race, Ethnicity, and the Achievement Syndrome," *American Sociological Review* 24 (1959): 47-60.
(18) Matthew Holden, "Education for Black Power," (Detroit: Wayne State University, 1967), p. 13. (mimeographed).
(19) *Ibid.*, p. 19.

V

The Quest
for Meaningful
Black Experience
on White Campuses

William J. Wilson

Black students' recent efforts to enrich their experiences on white campuses have generated a number of complex issues that require serious consideration by those of us committed to bringing about needed institutional changes. Many thoughtful and sensitive persons are addressing themselves to these issues, especially those dealing with the unanticipated consequences of certain efforts by white universities to meet the demands of black students. Vincent Harding, in a passionate and thought-provoking letter to black students and faculty in the North discussed these consequences insofar as they relate to the black community. (1) In the process of this discussion Harding seriously challenged the legitimacy of creating special programs designed to effect a more meaningful black experience on predominantly white campuses. In Harding's own words, his letter was "written in the spirit of black ecumenical concern as we move toward a new humanity," and he encouraged those of us to whom his remarks were directed to respond. As a black professor on a predominantly white campus, and one who has been involved in the kinds of programs under attack, I would like to take this occasion to detail my reaction to Professor Harding's very provocative letter. If I understand the basic points of his argument, he maintains:

1) That white northern institutions, as a result of black student pressure, have recently discovered the need to enroll more black

Reprinted with permission from *The Massachusetts Review* (Autumn, 1969): 737-746.

students, to hire more black faculty, and to establish various levels of black-oriented curricula; and in attempting to deal with this problem they have begun to exploit black schools in the South by recruiting competent black faculty, by entering "into serious competion with the southern schools for the best black students," and by pirating "some Afro-American curriculum which has not been destroyed by 'integration'."

2) That such activities are threatening the survival of black institutions because they are not in a position to compete effectively in terms of the fabulous scholarship and financial aids offered to the best black students, and the attractive salary figures, assistance for research and other inducements extended to black faculty.

3) That black students and faculty of northern institutions are participating fully in this common destruction (common in the sense that their activities circumvent the concept of the Black University and impede the development of new levels of black solidarity), not only by demanding the enrollment of more black students, the recruitment of black faculty and the establishment of black studies programs, but also by helping to raid black schools to meet their demands.

4) That serious questions can be raised about the fruitfulness of such demands and the contradictions they entail, e.g., if only a few institutes in Afro-American Studies "can live with significant integrity, where should they develop?", and would it not "make more sense to bring 50 black students to a black-oriented professor in the South than to take him away from his campus?"

5) That a program of action to deal with these problems and "make it possible for us to serve—rather than destroy—each other" includes: a) establishing special visiting professorships "rather than raiding of black schools"; b) creating a consortium in which one or more black and one or more white schools would pool their funds and jointly participate in the recruitment of black students and thereby provide each student the choice of spending three years at a black institution and a year at a white institution or vice versa; c) encouraging white institutions "to make long term substantial [financial] investments in the black academic institutions"; and d) organizing institutes to train future teachers of black studies programs at black colleges; especially those black schools having the resources to launch an institute immediately, e.g., the Atlanta University Center.

Since it is my intention to challenge Professor Harding on several points of a fundamental nature, I should like to begin with a brief statement of the no less important arguments with which I find myself in general accord. I agree with Professor Harding that the frantic search by white college administrators for black faculty, if left unchecked, will threaten the survival of black schools, and that many northern black students and faculty are either consciously or unconsciously contributing to this precarious state of affairs. Moreover, I agree that questions may be raised about the practicality of some northern students' demands and the contradictions they entail. Furthermore, I agree that a program of action is needed to correct this unfortunate situation.

My areas of disaccord pertain to a number of Harding's specific criticisms and recommendations, and, more importantly, his tendency to altogether ignore or to treat in a cursory fashion certain very crucial matters pertaining to the black higher education crisis.

Let me begin by amplifying this point as it specifically relates to the recruitment of black students. If those of us who are involved in increasing the enrollment of black students on northern white campuses were committed to the view that we should only search for the so-called "best" black students, Harding's arguments would have an unshakable foundation and we would be forced to seriously reappraise our efforts. Although Harding seems to confine his remarks to the elitist segment of the black student population, I do not know of any massive recruitment campaign which has been designed to enroll hundreds of black students each year that restricts itself in this manner. On the contrary, in response to, or in anticipation of, black student demands, northern colleges have developed a proliferation of programs directed toward enrolling "high risk" black students. Attempts to discourage such efforts would, in the final analysis, be catastrophic for the hundreds of thousands of denied black students who were, until recently, virtually ignored by institutions of higher learning. These were the forgotten black students from impoverished backgrounds—concentrated in northern ghettoes—who did not meet the entrance requirements of nearby state colleges, or did not have the financial resources to attend open door black colleges in the South. In fact, black students who lived in the South had a greater chance of entering colleges than those living in the North. For instance, we know that in 1965 approximately 30 percent of the black high school graduates in the South enrolled in institutions of higher learning (mostly black schools). (2) In the North however (except in the state of California which has a large number of open door junior colleges), the situation for black students was critical.

I would like to focus briefly on the New England area, for here the critical state of black higher education throughout the North is most forcefully exemplified. In 1965-66 there were only 2,216 blacks, or 0.69 percent of the total population, enrolled in the colleges, junior junior colleges and universities in New England. (3) Because the few black students attending New England colleges at that time represented largely the managerial and professional segments of the black population, one author was led to conclude ". . . that as far as the economically and socially depressed main body of American

Negroes are concerned, it would not matter at all if New England colleges and universities closed their doors tomorrow." (4) Black students' demands have helped to produce stepped-up recruitment efforts, and although the figure is still pitifully low, there are more black students enrolled in colleges in the state of Massachusetts in 1968-69 (3,019) than there were in all of New England in 1965-66. And, the Massachusetts figure is expected to dramatically increase over the next few years. For example, at the University of Massachusetts we expect to have nearly a thousand black students by the fall of 1970—most of whom will come from the ghettoes of Springfield and Boston. We are not recruiting students who would ordinarily go to black schools in the South but students who would have difficulty enrolling in any college. In fact, there are presently several "high risk" students on our campus who were outrightly rejected by black schools because they did not meet the conventional entrance requirements.

The emphasis on increasing the enrollment of black students is certainly not restricted to the state of Massachusetts. Large state universities and colleges in the North are conducting expansive recruitment campaigns in the ghettoes, some enrolling as many as 600 black students a year. These programs, moreover, 1) assist students in getting admitted to college, 2) provide financial support needed to attend college, and 3) furnish academic assistance needed to stay in college.

In the past, denied black students were measured by the same academic criteria that were applied to other students. No recognition was given to the crippling influence of ghetto schools, and as a result these students were usually rated as academically marginal at best. However, being marginal in these respects may not be a measure of a student's potential or intellect, it may merely indicate that he does not meet the conventional white middle-class standards of admission. (5) Therefore, it is incumbent upon black students and faculty in the North to continue to pressure their respective universities to abandon the system of recruiting only the "best" students (which ultimately leads them to search for students in the South). I think it is ludicrous for black recruiters from, say, Northwestern University to go all the way to Atlanta, Georgia, searching for black students, when there are thousands of black students in the ghettos of nearby Chicago just itching for a chance to enroll in college.

As northern universities continue to recruit the forgotten black students of the ghetto, it is conceivable that in the very near future, and unless an equally concerted effort is made in the South, a majority of black students will be concentrated in these institutions. And I would be hard pressed indeed to tell a black faculty member who was recruited expressly to satisfy the needs of these students that he should recognize his "true" obligation and teach in a black institution. As the enrollment figures of northern black students continue to mount, their needs cannot be denied. However, I do not feel that in order to satisfy the needs of increasing numbers of black students in the North, black schools in the South should suffer. It is for this reason that careful consideration should be given to Professor Harding's suggestions. I shall discuss this matter presently.

I was pleased to see Harding at least acknowledge the fact that many faculty and administrators at "predominantly Negro" colleges have been reluctant to grant "that our experience as a people was worthy of serious academic exploration." In the final analysis, this obstacle has to be overcome if Harding's suggestions are to be seriously entertained. Only a few black schools have the orientation which would permit immediate implementation of his proposals. We cannot ignore the rigid resistance to change described by Nathan Hare, Gwendolyn Midlo Hall, and others who have taught in traditionally oriented Negro colleges. (6) The reaction of entrenched black administrators to the recent student uprisings on these campuses is further evidence of their generally conservative atmosphere. Ironically, it is these schools that provide a good deal of the opposition to the Black University concept and to the creation of Afro-American curricula. (It is additionally ironic that the administrators of "predominantly Negro" schools have now been forced to recognize that they do indeed possess a valuable commodity in their black professor. Although they are unable to compete with rich white schools for his services, they may now find it necessary to at least give him the same rewards they have traditionally given to their white professor.) I recognize that Professor Harding did not address himself specifically to this issue, but it comes up time and time again in a critical assessment of his proposed solutions, to which I now turn.

"Considering our sadly limited resources," Harding states, "can there be more than a few really excellent programs or institutes of Afro-American Studies?" No doubt many of the premature black studies programs will fail if for no other reasons than a lack of qualified personnel to staff them and a lack of commitment on the part of white administrators to keep them in operation. It is thus imperative that a Black Studies Department have the kind of instructional personnel that would provide it with at least the same status as the very best departments on campus. If strong efforts are not made to enhance the quality of black studies programs on white campuses, they will have marginal status, and be subject to constant invidious academic distinctions. We cannot dismiss this problem as irrelevant. A marginal program will not attract qualified personnel regardless of their availability, and it will certainly experience difficulty in receiving budgetary supports, including research and planning grants from outside agencies. Such a situation in turn is bound to increase frustrations among black students. They may be able to improve matters momentarily by applying pressure, but the application of pressure resources is time and energy consuming. And as soon as the pressure is relaxed, the students will lose their leverage and the program may fail to progress as rapidly as necessary to eliminate the stigma of inferiority. These are serious problems that demand a thoughtful and creative formula. We may quickly dismiss, therefore, Harding's rhetorical suggestion that it might "make more sense to bring 50 black students to a black-oriented professor in the South than to take him away from his campus." If institutions in the North continue to enroll thousands of black students, it would be physically impossible to ship all or even a majority of them to the South, considering the limited space and resources of southern black schools. Only a small percentage of the total number of black students in the North would be able to take advantage of this opportunity, thereby creating a most unfortunate situation for those who are forced to remain. Moreover, unless the receiving southern institutions are "black oriented" we would be exposing the already "up-tight" northern black students to the traditionally oriented Negro colleges which, as I emphasized above, have yet to acknowledge the legitimacy of black studies programs. However, Professor Harding's suggestion of visiting professorships for southern black teachers in northern institutions is a feasible temporary solution to this problem. I emphasized the word 'temporary' because I am convinced that even with such visiting professorships the demand for black professors far exceeds the available supply. And the gap will rapidly widen. It cannot be denied, however, that this suggestion would provide a way of alleviating the pressure on white administrators and lessen their frantic search for permanent black professors. As a stop-gap solution then, the visiting professorship program should be immediately implemented. An arrangement could be made with white institutions to hold a moratorium on the recruitment of permanent black faculty from the South in favor of visiting black professorships (with the proviso that these institutions be permitted to hire as permanent faculty those black professors who personally initiate such an appointment). I should think that, if assured of the participation of black faculty in this regard, white administrators would be willing to cooperate. In this connection, Harding's recommendation that white institutions "make long term substantial [financial] investments in the black institutions" can be realistically entertained. More specifically, our historic experiences in this society should certainly make us aware of the fact that when men have to choose between protecting their own interests or preserving the interests of others, they almost invariably decide in favor of themselves. Altruism, regardless of how justified, rarely plays a major role in *important* decisions. (7) Black people, in their interactions with whites, have painfully found this proposition to be universally true. Accordingly, in order to assure long term commitment, white institutions must be made to recognize that they have a vested interest in financially supporting various endeavors in black institutions. For example, in return for an agreement to financially support research programs in certain black institutions, white institutions might receive the cooperation of black professors in accepting visiting professorships to staff their black studies departments. Such an arrangement would be healthier from the black colleges' point of view since it would eliminate the patronizing and condescension which invariably accompanies unilateral white donations or gifts.

Although the above suggestions would help preserve the black institutions and reduce some of the pressure on white institutions to recruit permanent black faculty, the long-range problem of the shortage of black faculty still remains. Therefore we should take a critical look at Professor Harding's suggestion that Afro-American institutes to train future teachers of black studies programs should be organized on black campuses.

Harding is correct in asserting that the Atlanta University Center has the potential manpower and resources to become the model for such a training institute. Colleges and foundations around the country would be well advised to make substantial financial investments in helping to organize and fully staff an institute which is designed to provide a significant percentage of the future teachers of black studies. However, I seriously question whether or not more than a handful of black institutions could launch an institute that would even remotely approximate the Atlanta Center model.

Since an overwhelming majority of major colleges or universities (and also a significant number of minor ones, including junior colleges) are establishing or contemplating the establishment of black studies programs, the demand for black faculty will reach extreme proportions. I am not convinced that the concentration of good graduate programs on a few well-equipped (in terms of staff, library resources, etc.) black campuses will ultimately satisfy this demand. We need only consider the fact that even with hundreds of graduate training programs in other disciplines, e.g., sociology, English, etc., the supply of college teachers is still limited. It is therefore inevitable, if a black studies program is to become a permanent fixture in our academic curricula, that graduate training centers also be organized at appropriate white institutions. I acknowledge that we run the risk of jeopardizing the integrity of black studies graduate departments by establishing them on white campuses, but I think that there are ways of reducing such risks. The most appropriate way would be to press that a black professor head each of these graduate institutes to insure that the black experience is meaningfully incorporated. He would, among other things, organize the curricula and screen out those professors, white or black, who do not have a proper orientation. Let me amplify this point.

I do not think we can ignore the fact that a black studies program, be it graduate or undergraduate, calls for teachers who are sensitive to the complex forces of race in our society and who have the psychological, sociological and historical imagination which would permit the most comprehensive interpretation and analysis of materials related to black experience. Moreover, I do not think that teachers who possess these qualities are solely or necessarily black. No doubt many white professors (and a great many black professors as well) do not have the orientation, training and experience needed to offer a meaningful course in black studies. But to assume that all white professors fall into this category is to go beyond the depths of reason. In view of our sadly limited resources, black studies programs would be jeopardized if competent, sensitive, in short "together," white professors, who could impart useful knowledge to black students, were excluded. But, to repeat, there are risks involved in choosing white professors, and it would have to be the responsibility of the black professor heading one of these training institutes to carefully select teachers who could make meaningful and significant contributions. It is obvious then that a number of key black professors would have to play major roles in organizing graduate training institutes on white campuses. I acknowledge that this suggestion further complicates the already acute shortage of black professors and might increase the black brain drain from southern colleges, but we could still retain the idea of the visiting professorship for non-headship positions in these graduate training institutes and recruit black professors from northern institutions for the headship positions.

Finally, in regard to the recruitment of black students, Harding's proposal of a consortium is a good one. However, certain qualifications should be introduced. Considering the fact that tens of thousands of black students in the North will be attending college as a result of the accelerating recruitment campaign, the consortium model could not be instituted across the board. If all black students were confronted with the consortium proposal and a substantial percentage decided to spend three of their four years at a black institution, where could we conceivably find the space to accommodate them? This question is very appropriately applied to the massive recruitment efforts of some large state universities that could enroll, say, 500 black students with little or no difficulty. It might be wise, therefore, to restrict the consortium idea to small white private schools and black colleges. For example, a school such as Morehouse in cooperation with Amherst College could accept fifty students who decide to spend three years on the Morehouse campus, but it would not have the space to accommodate the 700 black students to be enrolled in the fall of 1969 at San Fernando Valley State College in California. Moreover, recruitment programs organized by state institutions are generally based on state funds and their use and distribution have certain built-in limitations; northern private colleges, on the other hand, could easily use their funds to finance a student's three-year stay at a black institution. Furthermore, it would appear that the most successful programs of this nature would be those that involved southern schools with a black orientation and white schools with Afro-American curricula. In short, the consortium idea, although a good one, has limited application.

One last consideration. There is some indication that black students at a few white institutions are pressing for the establishment of separate branches of their respective institutions in the black community. These divisions, they argue, should be designed to meet the needs of the black community, organized and controlled by black students and financed by their white institution. If such developments should take place, scholar-oriented black studies programs will likely have as their major role the education of white students. On the other hand, black students will move beyond mere cultural and intellectual development in black studies and will spend a significant portion of their academic career in a Black University. As Fuller describes it, "the Black University will seek to involve the total black community and its institutions in a system of interrelated and interlocking 'schools' and programs of study which are designed to serve the black community in its reach toward unity, self-determination, the acquisition of political and economic power, and the protection of the freedom of the human spirit." (8) As the push for the concept of the Black University proceeds, it is very likely that the needs of black students on white campuses will be redefined and a gradual dissatisfaction with a black studies program that is not in some way directly and significantly involved with the black community will emerge. It could very well be, then, that the next chapter in our tense struggle will be a move from the scholar-oriented black studies program on white campuses to a community-oriented Black University. Accordingly, rather than undermining the concept of the Black University, as Harding suggests, it is quite possible that the proliferation of black studies programs could, in the long run, contribute to its ultimate realization.

Notes

(1) Vincent Harding, "New Creation or Familiar Death: An Open Letter to Black Students in the North," *Negro Digest* XXVIII (March 1969): 5-14.
(2) S. A. Kendrick, "The Coming Segregation of Our Selective College," *College Board Review,* No. 66 (Winter 1967-68): 6-13.
(3) *Ibid.*
(4) *Ibid.,* p. 6
(5) For an interesting discussion of these points, see Bill Somerville, "Can Selective Colleges Accommodate the Disadvantaged? Berkeley Says 'Yes'," *College Board Review,* No. 65 (Fall, 1967): 5-10.
(6) See Nathan Hare, "Final Reflections On A 'Negro' College." *Negro Digest* XXVII (March 1968), pp. 40-46 and 70-76; and Gwendolyn Midlo Hall, "Rural Black College," *Negro Digest* XXVIII (March 1969): 59-65.

(7) For an excellent discussion of this argument, see Gerhard Lenski, *Power and Privilege: A Theory of Social Stratification* (New York: McGraw-Hill, 1966), Chapter II.

(8) Hoyt W. Fuller, "Editor's Note," *Negro Digest* XXVIII (March 1969): 4, 95.

VI

An Analysis of Objectives of Institutes and Departments of Afro-American Affairs

Lamar P. Miller

All educational programs and the resulting organizational structures rest upon some implicitly or explicitly agreed upon ideological or philosophical notion. Black studies, however, presents a dilemma because it is part of a social cataclysm which perceives agencies and institutions as carriers of racism. Morever, the typical American view of education as a healer of great social divisions is seriously challenged by the goals and objectives of a university unit such as An Institute of Afro-American Affairs. It is this peculiar circumstance, which is far from settled, that sets the state for the analysis presented here. This chapter will discuss Ideological and Philosophical Perspectives, An Overview of Present Practice, Major Problems for Institutes Departments, and Centers, and Realistic Objectives for the Future.

Although there are differences in opinions as to what should be the goals of black studies programs, some evaluation and overview must be made. Admittedly, an objective assessment of established programs is difficult because of the many variations in stated purposes and organizational patterns of programs. But if we are to suggest future programs that are educationally valid, it is imperative that we examine the current state of affairs. Clearly, the most important consideration is whether or not such programs can assist the black man in his attempt to control his own life and thus contribute to the improvement of the black community and at the same time, help the white majority to develop an understanding of the absolute necessity for cultural pluralism.

There are few parallels in the history of American education that rival the dramatic emergence of black studies and the resulting developmental structures such as Institutes of Afro-American Affairs. As is true of most movements, the emphasis upon knowledge about and appreciation of Afro-Americans is not new, for many black writers and educators have promulgated such ideas for many years. Daniel (1) has suggested that most educators have little knowledge of the large number of black and white scholars who have been concerned with the history of blacks in American society and who have endeavored to secure for Afro-Americans, and their history and literature, a respected place in American education. In any case the contemporary movement is characterized by the concept that the black experience provides a context broader than the traditional study of history and literature.

Strangely enough, the impetus came not so much from the academics but from black students. It has been more than a decade since black college students took to the streets to swell the multitudes of concerned citizens who shouted "free by '63." During that time predominantly white institutions had been busy recruiting more minority group students to their campuses. Black students came in numbers, only to find themselves in some sort of foreign territory. But what was more alarming to them was that they were in the midst of an academic environment that gave little consideration to their most immediate concerns: eradicating racism, rectifying the omissions of history and helping their poor black brothers in the rotting cores of our great cities. Out of their frustrations in an historic academic environment came the cry for "a relevant education." In the main this cry was heard on predominantly white campuses. This does not mean that black colleges and universities have not also followed suit in the tradition of getting on the academic band wagon; even so, the assault may be characterized as blacks attacking white racist institutions. Students enrolled in predominantly black colleges have demanded black studies when and to the extent that they perceive these institutions to be replicas of their white counterparts.

The demand for black studies, in the opinion of many, is a manifestation of discontent with the present system. Indeed, the movement has achieved its current priority on a great many college campuses primarily as an outgrowth of protest by black students. The existence of black studies at most schools came from black students' struggles and their participation in the quest for a reordering of university priorities, despite strong opposition from university faculties. In fact, gains in terms of black studies programs were often attained only by confrontation; for example, the occupation of buildings, and demonstrations designed to get publicity and to force administrators to make favorable decisions.

Ideological and Philosophical Perspectives

Perhaps the most salient point to be made is that almost all of the early writings and discussions on black studies were concerned with the ideological and/or philosophical focus of the new programs. Black studies was seen by many as based primarily on an ideology of revolutionary nationalism with liberation and self-determination for black people as the ultimate goal. While many people, black and white, rejected this extreme view, those who have raised the black power thesis saw black studies as a training ground for leaders of the black revolution. Recognizing the need for the analysis of social, political, and economic conditions affecting black people, they gave highest priority to the action aspect of the black studies program—action which would lead to black separation by revolutionary means. At the other extreme were those who saw the introduction of black studies as a means of peaceful change and reconciliation. Between these positions other views characterized by greater moderation and balance developed, and the result has been the proliferation of individual black studies programs, with each institution determining the unique form and substance of its own efforts in this field.

In view of these divergent views it is easy to understand why during the past three years the subject of Afro-American Studies has been highly publicized and debated with considerable vigor. Critics and advocates from almost every academic discipline within the university and from almost every occupation outside of higher education reacted to the lively questions that were asked about the nature and proper place of black studies in higher education.

When this seemingly new area of study was started in several of the colleges and universities in this country, the advocates were called "ineffectual scholars," para-intellectuals or enemies of the university as a center for serious scholarship and the critics doubted whether black studies should have a place in the university curriculum. At first they resisted changes in the curriculum as they confused such changes with the lowering of standards. They were accordingly suspicious of any divergence from the traditional American pattern of education and saw black studies as the first step towards disarming them intellectually. To neglect Max Weber and Thomas Jefferson and substitute DuBois and Franz Fanon frightened them; to neglect racist history in favor of objective historical reinterpretation troubled their consciences; to regard all traditions of blacks as legitimate materials for scholarship; to take seriously the pre-colonial political and social institutions of Africa; to reflect on the cosmological ideas of Africa; these were threats to the critics of black studies. They did not see black studies institutes or departments as centers for stimulating the ferment of thought and serious scholarship.

Certainly no one can question the general seriousness of those who either initiated or advocated programs nor is there any doubt about the discontent among blacks with higher education and commitment to developing black studies programs. The fact is, however, that by the fall of 1971 many programs had either been phased out or had their activities severely curtailed. It is, therefore, not surprising that in some quarters it is being said that the questions that were asked two or three years ago about the nature of black studies have been answered and that it is time to put this issue aside for more up-to-date and debatable topics. On the other hand, there are those who maintain that the major issues have not been resolved, and new questions are surfacing more rapidly than old ones can be disposed of.

While the present evidence and current trends seem to indicate a lack of interest on the part of colleges and universities in the continued development of black studies programs, interested scholars need to continue their efforts to establish evidence based on sound logic that will make the necessity of such programs irrefutable. If colleges and universities are serious in their efforts to establish institutes and departments of Afro-American Affairs, and if they wish to continue to develop black studies as an academic discipline, they will have to recognize the obvious fact that the real issue pervading any discussion of the field centers around racism in American life. It is racism that has caused our educational system to fail in the most fundamental way to provide educational experiences that are relevant to blacks. It is racism which dictates not only the choice of materials to be presented and the way they are presented, but also the way black students' problems are perceived and dealt with by teachers and professors.

The understanding of racism as a principle acknowledges that special relationship which continues to exist between blacks and whites as evidenced by generally separate communities, different ways of life and the co-existence of two Americas, one white, one black. The fact that we manage to maintain this unique way of life is crucial to an understanding of racism and should form a basic rationale for the conduct of black studies.

An important related principle is that the whole range of perceptions of black people which revolves around the effect of racism is negative. Thus, black and white perspectives of the same phenomena are often different. Recent polls continue to point out that white people generally believe that blacks have tried to move too fast and that black people believe progress has been too slow. Clearly, history in America is perceived by black America differently from the way in which white America has largely portrayed that history. Such differences in perspective are not accidental but are derived from two separate systems of ordering knowledge.

What the above concept implies relates to the entire aspect of differential experiences. Lerone Bennett, Jr., at a meeting of the Institute of the Black World in Atlanta, Georgia in 1969, gave a stirring analysis of this subject. One of his main points was that perhaps the slave and the slave master, because of the qualitative differences in the nature of their experiences, lived in different existential times. His observation suggests that even though you and I share the same physical space, unless there is some similarity in the nature of our mutual experiences, we may well live in different times. Ronald Walters suggests that:

If one were able to look at these differential experiences over time, then one could clearly discern a pattern, a rhythm of events in the black community which may well have been different than the accumulation of important events in the white community. The point is that when we refer to the black perspective, we are speaking of a different order—a different reality—a different history. It is important to understand that for the times in which we live, these concepts refer to different people with different imperatives for the future. (2)

Indeed, the Afro-American experience is a profoundly unique experience. In May, 1969, the American Council on Education sent its member institutions a special report on the increasingly controversial subject of "Black Studies Programs and Civil Rights." In the report it was conceded that black studies and Afro-American studies, or a term like the black perspective, are understood variously. It is quite clear that white society and many white scholars did not seem to understand either the uniqueness, the diversity, or the meaning of the black experience.

Undoubtedly in summarizing the preceding remarks, much of the hesitancy with which educators have met demands for the inclusion of black studies in the curriculum arises from an ignorance of the black experience and the difference in perspective. This is perhaps the basic reason for resistance in educational circles to black studies programs. There are, however, two related concerns. First, many educators question the moral responsibility involved in complying with public pressures for curriculum reforms. They worry lest they might be deserting their obligation to maintain high standards of excellence in curriculum offerings by responding favorably to insistent protests from local groups. Second, many educators seriously question the assertion that the experiences of black people in Africa and in the United States are subjects of sufficient amplitude and depth to justify general study and instruction on all educational levels.

The rhetoric of almost all such reservations is phrased in intellectual terms, with questions about matters of academic responsibility or the intellectual defensibility of using black issues and themes as a basis for instruction, rather than granting the possibility that there are things worth teaching of which even most academicians may be unaware. One might even suggest that the unwillingness to admit that even educators may be ill-informed about vitally important issues is symptomatic of the many problems of educational institutions in contemporary America.

An Overview
of Present Practice

In the previous section we pointed out the importance of ideological and philosophical perspectives and we drew attention to the racism that pervades our educational system. We now turn our attention to the present status of Institutes of Afro-American Affairs and black studies departments. One could only hazard a reasonably intelligent guess about the actual numbers of the Afro-American Studies programs in the United States because there has been no systematic reporting of such programs. In some surveys attempts have been made to ascertain the number of programs, but what has been reported is a list of institutions that offer at least one course in Afro-American Studies. Moreover, most attempts to survey the field have not dealt with the basic issues which constitute a conceptional framework.

Nevertheless, a few surveys have been initiated by various individuals and institutions. In the process of proposing a structure for black studies at the University of Cincinnati, William D. Smith (3) conducted a survey of colleges and universities from all sections of the United States. The study included data from schools that were privately and publicly supported, had large and small enrollments, were attended by predominantly black and predominantly white pupils, were co-educational as well as all male and all female, and were religiously oriented and non-religiously oriented. Smith's study included 140 schools with varying types of academic structures or models. Table 12 illustrates the number of colleges and universities

TABLE 12
Structures for Afro-American Study Programs
in 140 Colleges and Universities[4]

School Categorized According to Report Models	Types of Academic Structure or Models	Percentage of Academic Structure or Models
7	Interdisciplinary Programs	5
8	Institutes	6
10	Centers	7
18	Departments	13
70	Afro-American courses only	50
27	No Afro-American courses	19
Total 140	Total	100

responding with different types of academic structures or models of Afro-American Study programs.

The data in Table 12 indicate that five models or trends for initiating black studies in colleges and universities have emerged. The most significant item was the large group of schools, 50 percent of those reporting, which indicated they had no programs and offer only formal courses. While this study has some shortcomings, it does indicate that there are relatively few formalized programs in Afro-American Studies.

A comprehensive study was also undertaken by the New York State Education Department in 1969. (5) This study represented a survey of all two- and four-year institutions in New York State. One-hundred twenty-four private colleges and universities in New York State, all of the State Universities (26 units) and 54 percent of the city university's four-year colleges responded. In all, 105 institutions reported offering either graduate or undergraduate courses in Afro-American Studies, and each institution projected an increase in the number of courses to be offered the following year. Again the trend was toward the offering of Afro-American courses rather than the development of formalized programs and organizational units.

M. A. Farber (6) indicated that there are at least 170 Black Studies programs in the nation. His estimate was based on conversations with black studies directors throughout the country. Further examination of the literature reveals that there are insufficient data to indicate the exact number of Afro-American Studies programs offered at universities throughout the country. The most intelligent guess that can be made here is that there are at least 200 Afro-American Studies programs and probably as many as 400 other institutions which offer courses in Afro-American Studies. For the most part, however, institutions have not coordinated their offerings into formal degree programs in the form of departments, centers, or institutes. Obviously, there is a need for more extensive and more accurate data concerning the extent of Afro-American Studies in the nation's colleges and universities.

Among those institutions of higher education which have Afro-American Studies programs, there appears to be wide variation in the organization and operation. This can be seen by an examination of ten recipients of Ford Foundation grants:

Atlanta University	Princeton University
Duke University	Rutgers University
Howard University	Stanford University
Lincoln University	Vanderbilt University
New York University	Yale University (7)

The reasons for the establishment of programs in these universities range from purely academic—the transmission of knowledge about the black experience—to a social emphasis, including actual academic work. While these are not the only schools in the country with well-organized and well-operated programs, they are representative. In the area of administration there is no uniform organizational pattern. Seven of the programs are interdepartmental. They use both existing courses offered by regular departments and new courses developed for the program, and they usually have a coordinating office which acts as an administrative center. Of the other three programs, two operate as institutes, and one functions as an independent department. This capsule view of interdepartmental programs in contrast with institutes, centers, and autonomous departments probably reflects a national pattern. We suspect, however, that the percentage of formalized programs organized by departments, institutes, or centers is even smaller than that suggested in this sample of ten.

A detailed description of organization structure at specific schools provides further insight. When the program is interdepartmental, usually a committee of faculty and students is formed which reflects the views of all departments involved. Stanford offers a good example of interdepartmental program organization.

The program is officially called The Undergraduate Program in African and Afro-American Studies. It is administered by a "Committee-in-Charge" appointed by the Dean of Humanities and Sciences, and is composed of representatives of each of the cooperating departments. It is the committee that "guarantee" the legitimacy of the degree. It does not meet, but members are consulted as individuals by the chairman who is an appointee of the University President. The Committee derives its authority from an Academic Senate. Curriculum planning and the details of negotiations with both the administration and the Black Students' Union concerning budget and other matters are in the hands of a steering committee. This committee is appointed annually by the Dean of Humanities and Sciences. The student members are designated as follows: two by the Black Students' Union, one by the African Students Association and one by the Associated Stanford Students' Union. The faculty members are appointed directly by the Dean in consultation with the Chairman. During the 1969-70 session, the Steering Committee was composed of four black students, three black faculty members and two white faculty members. (8)

New York University's Institute of Afro-American Affairs represents a different approach to Afro-American Studies. It is basically an autonomous Institute functioning in cooperation with the various colleges and units of the University. There are three major functions of the institute: education, research, and library, archives and educational services. The education program includes formal and informal activities in social sciences, the creative arts, and the professional arts. The focus is on broad academic areas that have relevance to the needs of black people, while at the same time maximizing flexibility in the development of specific programs. Courses are developed jointly with the various schools and colleges of the university. This cooperative approach of working through the regular divisions of the university has the advantage of utilizing the entire range of scholarship present at the university in the study of the black experience.

Majors in various areas of black studies are coupled with a major in one of the academic disciplines. For example, black literature is handled through the English Department or Afro-American history through the History Department. Similar arrangements would apply to the establishment of a minor. Programs have been developed in both undergraduate and graduate areas. The School of Education, for example, offers a Master of Arts in Black Studies in Education. In each division of the university where a program involving black studies is to be conducted, an advisory committee composed of black students, black and white faculty and the Education Director of the Institute develops the basic sequence of courses and experiences which is subsequently referred to the faculty of the appropriate school for approval.

The Institute has been involved in a number of research and training activities which focus on increasing opportunities for black Americans. Programs funded by the U. S. Office of Education, designed to improve and increase the skills of minority group individuals in educational research, were conducted during the summers of 1970 and 1971. A number of informal education activities such as lectures and seminars are conducted by the Institute and a literary publication called *Black Creation* has achieved national recognition. The Institute at New York University is an example of a formalized structure which is the central body of the University concerned with Afro-American Studies. The approach is quite different from the inter-departmental structure and is therefore, atypical.

Gregory V. Rigsby states that, "Howard University has been a center for research and instruction relating to the black man's existence for more than half a century." (9) The program at this university is an example of the departmental structure. The faculty of the Liberal Arts College, prodded by student demands, voted in 1968 to establish a department of Afro-American Studies within the College of Liberal Arts. The department has three basic divisions: historical surveys, cultural studies, and contemporary problems. The basic idea at Howard is to expand the Afro-American Studies department until it expresses DuBois' idea of the Black College. In 1933 W. E. B. DuBois, during an address at commencement week at Fisk University, said:

Starting with present conditions and using the facts and the knowledge of the present situation of American Negroes, the Negro university expands toward the possession and the conquest of all knowledge. It seeks . . . from a beginning of social development among Negro slaves and freedom in America and Negro tribes and Kingdoms in Africa, to interpret and understand the social development of all mankind in all ages . . . it cannot start with sociology, and lead to Negro sociology. (10)

DuBois' approach to black studies is inductive—from the particular to the universal; thus Howard is concerned with a college where every discipline is geared toward giving to black people guidance for action so that college bred students will be able to apply their knowledge to solving the problems peculiar to the black man in America and throughout the world. Howard University's program is not only an example of a departmental structure, but one which is based on a concrete philosophy. While their current program is not structured along the lines DuBois envisioned, there is a belief that a black studies program can be fashioned to be the embryo of a Black College.

The Afro-American Studies Department at Harvard University, while departmental, is an approach to black studies that is somewhat different than that at Howard University. The program is basically designed to develop the Afro-American identity by studying the black experience. It has a heavy emphasis on courses related to the study of Africa and its people such as African language, literature, politics and religion. There are courses on the slave trade, but not slavery, and on black culture in the Carribean. Apparently Harvard leans toward the academic rather than the missionary function of black studies. Their program is typical of white universities who prefer to emphasize the African experience rather than the Afro-American experience.

There are, of course, other types of organizations and structures that focus directly on Afro-American Studies or have at least a related function. North Carolina A & T State University, for example, sought to develop a regional center for Afro-American Studies. Probably the only difference between the idea of a center and that of an institute, in this case at least, is the effort to establish a regional approach. Some schools, such as Michigan State University, have established centers for Urban Affairs which seek to focus university resources on the problems of urban America. Some of these centers, however, have a strong emphasis on the development of programs that are similar to the approach to Afro-American Studies as evidenced by institutes and departments. The center at Michigan State is committed to the development of a socially relevant curriculum. A number of black studies courses such as Black literature, and music are offered in cooperation with specific departments.

In summary, while there appears to be no uniform organizational pattern for programs, most have much in common. As we suggested earlier most programs grew out of struggles initiated by black students. While the form did not come from a commonly agreed upon blueprint, in one way or another most programs have been intimately concerned with black students and their activities. This concern evidently did not satisfy black students because they continued to stress their desire to remain autonomous by maintaining separate student organizations. The Afro-American Student Centers at New

York University and Harvard are examples of organizations run by students on campuses where there are formalized black studies units.

Although the organizational patterns are similar, despite differences in official titles, there are some major differences in programs. A few have been committed to the development of community relations while others are strictly academic. Among those emphasizing academic programs, some focus on primarily African courses while others are Afro-American. In addition some schools have combined opportunity programs for university students with Afro-American Studies. In these schools there is a strong emphasis on helping students improve their academic work by providing counseling and tutorial services. In any case, the development of Afro-American Studies programs has been slow. A few schools have made major advances and have demonstrated that these programs can be successful, but most institutions are still struggling with the question of the feasibility of establishing Afro-American Studies programs.

Major Problems for Institutes, Departments, and Centers

Now that we have some idea of the magnitude and scope of black studies programs in the United States and have looked briefly at their organization and structure, we need to examine some of the major problems and prospects for colleges and universities. Perhaps the most obvious difficulty is that of providing an adequate staff of qualified faculty. The most common explanation of this difficulty is the failure of American institutions to train individuals with specific competence in areas such as black literature, history and anthropology. More specifically the proglem is one of finding black professionals who have the background and experience necessary to teach in such programs. Comparatively few scholars, black or white, have strong concentrations with regard to preparation in these areas. This is not to overlook, of course, outstanding scholars such as John Hope Franklin, Benjamin Quarles, C. Eric Lincoln, Carter G. Woodson and a host of other contemporaries who have devoted their careers to areas of black studies. The fact is that it is difficult to find black professors who meet the educational requirements demanded by most universities. While there have been a variety of explanations of the difficulty, the most obvious observation is that the problem is one of supply and demand. There are probably fewer than 3,000 black Ph. D.'s in the entire country. In fact, blacks constitute less than two percent of all Ph. D.'s in American education. But no one really knows how many of these have both the interest and the necessary preparation to teach in black studies areas.

Universities and colleges with effective programs have developed a number of ways of working around the difficult staffing problem. They include making joint faculty appointments between the black studies institutes and centers and other departments; sharing faculty with other schools and universities and bringing in outside experts and community leaders as guest lecturers.

A number of white institutions have recognized the difficulty in attracting faculty not only because of the limited supply, but also because the ideological image of their institutions is often unattractive to black scholars. Moreover, the issue of the brain drain, or white institutions raiding black schools for faculty, has not become the dilemma that many administrators predicted a few years ago. While one should not underestimate the severity of the current problems of black colleges and universities, there has been at least a slight trend in black professionals seeking positions and returning to black institutions. The shortage of staff, however, in specialized areas of black studies will in all probability continue to be a major problem.

Intrauniversity conflict concerning availability of faculty is as much a problem as the attempt to find staff outside the university. In those programs where staff members do not have departmental status it is difficult to gain promotion and tenure because the reward system is one place while the job is somewhere else. Morever, faculty members in traditional departments are often not convinced on the validity of black studies in an intellectual enterprise. The result is that individuals teaching and working in black studies areas have a difficult time gaining acceptance as professional equals among colleagues in their respective departments. To get some idea of how black studies programs are staffed, the numbers, degrees and fields of faculty specialization in ten programs are shown in Table 13.

Most universities require the doctorate degree for professional rank. Moreover, universities generally seek individuals who have specific training and expertise in a given field. Since the offering of programs with a concentration in such specialities as black history or black literature is a recent occurrence, the problem of staffing becomes even more complex. Fortunately, a number of black scholars who possess the doctorate in other fields along with a number of individuals with Master of Arts degrees have spent considerable time in acquiring the knowledge needed to teach in black studies areas. Nevertheless, if we are to fill positions available in colleges and universities around the country a substantial number of teachers will have to come from the young black scholars currently in graduate programs.

A second related problem cited by almost all program directors is

TABLE 13

Staffing of Black Studies Programs
in Ten Universities

Institution	Faculty Teaching in Program	Number from Other Depts.	Number Added Last Year	Number Adjunct	Degrees of Fields of Specialization
Duke	14		6		All Ph.D's in 8 depts.: English, history, economics, sociology, political science, psychology, divinity, music.
Princeton	39	26	3	2	Over 40 professors, associate and assistant professors, lecturers, visiting lecturers from many fields.
Stanford	15	15	4		4 Ph.D's in history, 3 in social anthropology, 2 in political science, 1 each in psychology and English, 2 Ph.D candidates, 1 history professor, 1 West Indian psychologist, 1 Ph.D visiting professor of history.
New York University	25-30	25-30			Regular Faculty; most hold doctorates.
Rutgers	14	14		2	Director-Ph.D candidate in political science, sociologist-Ph.D candidate.
Douglass College of Rutgers University	8	6	1	3	3 M.A.'s (art, music, literature) 2 Ph.D's (religion, history).
Howard	8	5			3 M.A.'s, 5 Ph.D's (economics, history, English literature, linguistics, speech, sociology).
Lincoln	1	1			Director-M.A. in psychology; faculty-1 M.A. in psychology; 1 director of student activities; 2 Ph.D's in political science.
Vanderbilt	22	22	2		All but one are Ph.D's; wide variety of fields.
Yale	20-25	20+	2 full-time 4 part-time	varies	Most are Ph.D's (excluding lecturers offering courses in the residential colleges).

funding. In view of the financial crisis in public and private institutions of higher education, this is not at all surprising. Nevertheless, budgets for black studies programs in 1971 ranged from a low of $57,000 per year to a high of $150,000. While most programs are supported by the parent institution, sources for funds include foundations and the U. S. Office of Education. The U. S. Office of Education has also provided grants for summer institutes. Since most universities are faced with drastic cuts in their operations, black studies programs, especially those conducted outside of regular departments, are faced with serious difficulties.

The problem of funding is obviously related to that of staffing since the biggest item is usually faculty salaries. Other items such as informal seminars, lectures and publications which can be vital to the success of a program may be curtailed in the very near future. On the other hand, a good many directors and department heads are optimistic and are seeking ways to circumvent their lack of resources. There appears to be a trend in urban centers where several colleges are located to divide the job among cooperating schools in order to prevent wasteful duplication and spread the sparse staff and money. In addition, some schools are sharing the cost of bringing scholars to the various campuses. In any case, the financial problem is generally school-wide and not just restricted to institutions with departments of black studies.

The third major problem is that of administration. Virtually all black studies program directors have faced a difficult challenge. In general, the director or chairman of a department, institute or center has had the same responsibility as any college department chairman: recruiting, developing and training staff, budgeting and funding, conceptualizing, implementing and evaluating the program. Indeed the uniqueness of these programs has meant that directors have had a host of other responsibilities such as developing curriculum, advising students and responsibility for public relations. More often than not directors must devote time and effort toward overcoming existing institutional biases and inertia in black and white colleges by educating the faculty. Coupled with the continued pressure from black student groups, the tenure of administrators at most schools has been brief. The turnover during the past few years is understandably high because colleges have either asked too much of their black studies directors, or they have not given them adequate support. In most cases, they have been expected to do too much too fast, as well as to provide solutions to problems which required the resources of the total university.

While there are other issues, the problems of funding, staffing and administration are the most crucial. If institutions are to expect gradual but steady program growth, they will have to deal realistically with these problems. This will require a recognition of black studies as a viable and necessary part of university life.

Realistic
Objectives
for the Future

The preceding discussion is an overview of the developing discipline of black studies. The primary value of this chapter, however, is that hopefully it will provide some clues that will more clearly delineate the goals and objectives of institutes, departments, and centers as well as identify some of the more serious issues as defined by those individuals upon whom the success or failure of black studies rests.

Many of the issues considered here are those most often written about and debated at conferences and meetings around the country. Although there are still differences of opinion, some conclusions can be drawn. The organization of programs and, therefore, the objectives have been subjective rather than objective. The focus of programs depends on the philosophy of those conducting or planning programs. It was clear from the outset that critics and advocates alike were concerned with the ideology of black studies and that any attempt to discuss the question outside of this perimeter was futile. Accordingly, the general tenor of most opinions is an expression of strong feelings of beliefs and values.

Even though the development of programs is a result of highly publicized and dramatic black student struggles, only a few colleges and universities have instituted more than a few history courses which they have called black studies programs. And of those that have mounted substantial programs there still remain areas of contention as to what the programs should include. Students are not even sure what it is they want, other than to participate in the decision-making process. And in too many instances students, once given this opportunity, fail to live up to their responsibility.

In general, blacks continue to feel that resistance results from ignorance of the black experience, but some believe that it is also due to the refusal of institutions to bend or to make adjustments in the present organization and on another level to recognize and admit that within the educational community for generations they had denied the past of black people. Still others are certain that the resistance to black studies is a question of values rather than a question of believing that there aren't enough scholarships around to draw from. The study of black art, literature, music and philosophy is just not deemed important by those responsible for curriculum development. Moreover, the uncertainty of the outcome of black studies is considered responsible for part of the resistance to it. From an organizational point of view, administrators are sometimes interested in having the answers to certain questions before they consent to adding anything more than a few history or literature courses—such questions as, will black studies educate or indoctrinate? Is it going to create more militancy? Is it part of a separatist trend that is taking place? Is it going to create an alliance of nationalism among black students? Indeed the paramount question is whether or not a black studies program should lean toward the academic or the missionary function as a goal.

Charles V. Hamilton provides an overview of possible objectives for black studies in the identification of six common elements or purposes which exist unevenly and often conflictingly. He suggests an ascending order beginning with the usual academic (or white) concept and progressing to the missionary or (black) impulse. His six common elements or purposes of black studies are:

1) The gap theory — black studies ought to fill gaps in our knowledge of history, sociology, literature etc.; 2) Training of black leaders in the traditional sense — educating them to think like white men and sending them back to keep the ghetto quiet; 3) Humanism — transcending black-white color conflicts by developing a culture of humanity; 4) Reconciliation—integration is involved here; 5) Pride in being black — based on the identity theme; 6) Ideology — politicization of students as black nationalists or nation building. (12)

Hamilton arrived at these objectives by examining some forty-one major proposals for black studies programs. He believes that a program ought to be academically sound and do more than add a few courses to the curriculum. A truly meaningful program, in his opinion, ought to raise entirely new empirical questions and challenge students to seek viable solutions to black problems.

Edmond V. Gordon (13) in discussing the components of black studies, defined them as: 1) Expansion of knowledge: 2) The reorganization of existing knowledge, and 3) Reconceptualization. The first seems substantially the same as Hamilton's gap theory, that is acquiring new knowledge of the history, etc., of black people. The second function can be illustrated by the two recent misuses of knowledge by white scholars such as D. P. Moynihan on the black family and A. R. Jensen on genetic inheritance. Gordon's reconceptualization appears to be like Hamilton's pride in being black. In addition he feels that economic and social problems will get solved as time passes and then living instead of making a living will become the primary interest. In this cultural growth black studies provide the basic knowledge and inspiration, as in the present crusade, still task oriented, but rearranged to serve different tasks.

The resolution of the problem of determining appropriate and realistic objectives for organizational units remains a task, but it represents a challenge that must not be ignored. The most realistic objectives that we can suggest in view of the history and strong emotions are:

1) The expansion of knowledge about blacks—to fill in the gaps in our knowledge of history, sociology, literature, etc.

2) The reorganization of knowledge—a more proper appraisal of existing knowledge about blacks.

3) The education of black students in divergent fields so that they may provide useful services to the black community as well as intelligent leadership.

4) Reconceptualization—development of programs and activities that foster pride in being black.

5) Humanizing—the reeducation of whites in an effort to bring about a new socialization process.

6) Alter the character of the university—assist the university in becoming a place where equality and freedom are a part of academic pursuit as well as everyday practice.

There are a number of individuals today who will argue that academia is not a place where new ideas originate, only where new ideas from elsewhere are legitimatized and disseminated. They argue further that black studies in the form of departments or institutes cannot change the universities. On the other hand, there are those who believe that academia, while it may be bad, is not all that bad and while often hostile, is still usable. But both groups agree that if any objectives at all are to be realized, the university is the place where we must at least make the effort.

These objectives are not original; in fact, if anyone should be given the credit it would be DuBois. This most certainly provides us with some assurance that we are headed in the right direction. Programs based on these objectives would go far beyond the necessary psychological value of self-identity for blacks. Such a program could broaden the professional student's insights so that he might have a different orientation about how to use his educational tools for the development of the black community and this society. It could be the frontier of explaining and exploring new forms of government in this society. It could search out with students new mechanisms of meaningful decision making that would understand alienation in the black community. It could be on the cutting edge of change and articulate new ways of ending exploitation and oppression in this society. In short it could provide a relevant functional education that is concerned with the way in which we utilize the disciplines, the professions, in the cultural development of people.

As we suggested earlier the most important issues with regard to the permanence of black studies in the university have not been raised, although the problems of administration, funding and staffing, and ideology are important and need continuous examination. The most fundamental question is whether or not black studies can inevitably alter the character of the university in the decades ahead so that our learning experiences are not directed primarily at helping people learn how to make a living, but toward helping people learn how to live together.

Notes

(1) Walter J. Daniel, "Black Studies in American Education," *Journal of Negro Education* 39 (1970): 189.
(2) Ronald W. Walters, "Philosophical Concepts in Black Education," a speech delivered at the conference on the Problems of Organization of Black Studies Programs, New York University, February, 1970.
(3) William D. Smith, "Black Studies; A Survey of Models and Curricula," *Journal of Black Studies* 1 (1971): 259-272.
(4) *Ibid.*, p. 262.
(5) The State Education Department, Information Center on Education. *Afro-American Studies in Colleges and Universities on New York State, 1968-69 and 1969-70,* (New York: University of the State of New York, 1970).
(6) M. A. Farber, "Black Studies Take Hold, But Face Many Problems," *New York Times* (December 27, 1970).
(7) Management Division of the Academy for Educational Development, *Black Studies: How It Works at Ten Universities,* (New York: Academy for Educational Development), 1971.
(8) *Ibid.*, p. 3.
(9) Gregory V. Rigsby, "Afro-American Studies at Howard University," *Journal of Negro Education,* 39 (1970): 3, 209.
(10) W. E. B. DuBois, "The Negro College," *Crisis* (August, 1933): 176.
(11) *Black Studies: How It Works at Ten Universities,* p. 5.
(12) Charles V. Hamilton, "The Question of Black Studies," *Phi Delta Kappa* 51 (1970): 362-364.
(13) Edmond V. Gordon, Address delivered at conference on the Organization and Problems of Black Studies in Higher Education, February, 1970.

VII

Higher Education
and Black Americans:
Implications for the Future

Edgar G. Epps

"Education is the corridor through which America's minorities move from rejection, deprivation, and isolation to acceptance, economic efficiency, and inclusion." (1) This quotation expresses a sentiment that is widely accepted by American social scientists. In spite of the fact that employment discrimination severely limits the earning power of college educated blacks in America when compared with college educated whites, the average lifetime earning power of black male college graduates is approximately twice that of black males with less than eight years of elementary school.

Recent census data indicate that in the last few years there has been a rapid increase in the returns blacks receive from investment in education. This increase is already being reflected in earning power. Unlike the situation of a few years ago, the gap between median black and white family incomes was smaller in 1968 for blacks with a year or more of college than it was for those with lesser amounts of education. The implication of this new trend is that the gap between blacks and whites will close most rapidly for those blacks who are fortunate enough to obtain one or more years of college education. Thus, it appears that the attainment of higher education will continue to be one of the most important requirements for occupational and economic success. (2)

College Attendance Rates

Larger proportions of black students from low income backgrounds will have to attend college if blacks are to attain educational parity with whites. What are the prospects for such an increase? We already know that low income students constitute an unusually large proportion of the total black college student population. Recent surveys (3) report that more than half of the black college students come from families with annual incomes of less than $6,000. Only about 15 percent of white college students report such low family incomes. How well do these low income students do when compared with other students in terms of dropout rates and academic achievement? The available information indicates that in predominantly black colleges low income students achieve at the same level as students from more comfortable circumstances. (4) Other research shows that while the grade point averages of black students at white colleges may be lower than those of white students, black students are only slightly more likely to become dropouts than whites. When viewed from this perspective, black students from low income backgrounds are not extremely risky prospects for higher education.

Although the bulk of the black students now in college come from low income backgrounds, the overall rate of attendance is still low relative to that of the white population. Data presented in census reports indicate that only 7 percent of the freshmen who entered college in 1969 were black. This proportion had increased slightly to 7.7 percent by the fall of 1970 (522,000 black students were enrolled in college during the fall of 1970). (5) Since twelve percent of the college age population is black, blacks are obviously underrepresented among college students. Even this low rate of attendance represents a tremendous improvement over the recent past. The U. S. Bureau of Census reported that black students in college increased by 110 percent between 1964 and 1969. (6) We must keep in mind, however, that much of this increase represents students who are in the early years of college and includes those in two-year colleges and those enrolled in non-credit courses as well as those in four-year institutions. Many of those in two-year colleges will not go on to become four-year college graduates, while many of the students in four-year colleges will become casualties due to academic, financial, or personal adjustment problems.

Graduation

Graduation from high school or college is much more important for low income persons than attendance without graduation. The black person with "some college" is no better off than the white person who is a high school graduate. Census reports for 1969 indicate that while 13.5 percent of black persons between the ages of 25 and 29 (compared to 32.1 percent of whites) had completed at least one year of college, only 6.6 percent of this age group had completed college (compared to 16.2 percent of whites). In other words, although attendance rates for blacks increased 110 percent between 1964 and 1969, a much greater increase would be needed to overcome the current underrepresentation of blacks among the college educated. The discrepancy is most serious at the level of college graduation. One of the most important questions about the recent increase in black enrollment in white colleges is: "How many will graduate?" How committed are white colleges and universities to the goal of providing the resources required to assure the complete education of most of the black students who are recruited and admitted?

The Role of Black Colleges

"Harvard College had been established nearly 225 years and Yale 125 years when the first Negro in the United States received his bachelor's degree. At the time of the Civil War in 1860 only 28 Negroes had been graduated from recognized colleges in the United States." (7) For most of the past 120 years, higher education for blacks has usually meant segregated education. As recently as 1968, 80 percent of the baccalaurate degrees awarded to blacks were earned at black colleges and universities. The same pattern has been true for professional training as well; the handful of professional schools founded for blacks have produced the majority of professionals. Only at the graduate level, in the awarding of master's and doctoral degrees, have the major institutions founded for whites produced the majority of black degree holders.

Since 1965, as a result of increased pressure from civil rights groups and the federal government, many of the traditionally white institutions have enrolled substantial numbers of black students. Recent reports indicate that black colleges and universities now enroll less than one-third of all black college students. This represents a considerable change in enrollment patterns since 1964 when 51 percent of black students were enrolled in the black colleges and universities. During that period, total college enrollment for blacks increased from about 234,000 to 522,000, while the enrollment at black colleges increased from 120,000 to 144,000. Therefore, it is clear that most of the increase in black student enrollment has taken place in non-black colleges.

Since substantial numbers of black students still attend the traditionally Negro colleges of the southern and border states, it is instructive to look at some data from these schools. *The Advancement Newsletter* (December, 1970) issued by the Office for Advancement of Public Negro Colleges reported that the 33 public institutions represented by the organization enroll approximately 104,000 students. They estimate that about 90 percent of these students are black. The white enrollment is concentrated in border state institutions, however, and very few deep south schools report white enrollments of five percent or more.

The United Negro College Fund represents 36 private institutions with a combined enrollment of 40,000 students. These colleges range in size from over 10,000 to less than 300 students. According to a recent press release, this represents 25 percent of enrollments in black colleges and 12 percent of black students enrolled in all colleges and universities. Traditionally, black private colleges have tended to be more selective academically than the public institutions, and their students have also tended to come from more affluent backgrounds. Therefore, it is these institutions which are feeling the greatest pinch from the competition with predominantly white colleges and universities. Rising costs have forced most institutions to raise tuition and fees. This increase in cost to students has not been balanced by an increase in financial aid available to assist needy students.

The majority of the students attending predominantly black colleges reside in the south. Most of the students are drawn from the state in which the college is located. When compared to a national sample of college students, the students who attend these schools report lower parental income, lower parental education, fewer college-bound students in their high school graduating classes, and less satisfaction with their high school preparation. Most of the parents are in non-professional occupations. It is not surprising, given these facts, that compared to a national sample, a smaller proportion of the students attending predominantly black colleges have their education fully supported by their parents. Additional financial aid for students is one of the most pressing needs of these colleges as larger proportions of low income high school graduates seek admission to college. The most pressing problem of low income students is that of finding enough money to complete their education. Already, some college presidents are faced with the fact that two-thirds of their students are supported by some type of financial aid administered by the college. In a survey of 10 southern black colleges conducted in 1965, a large proportion of the students who came from poverty level backgrounds were found to be financing their education almost entirely through some type of loan. Loans were three times as important for the poverty group as for students who reported family incomes of $6,000 or more per year. (8) Thus, their financial handicap follows low income students even after they graduate from college in the form of loans which must be repaid with cash or services.

As suggested earlier, the academic climate varies considerably among southern black colleges. Some of the more academically oriented schools send more than half of their graduates on to postgraduate education. Other schools send less than one-fourth to graduate school. The schools which send larger proportions to graduate school tend to be the private liberal arts colleges which were traditionally considered to be the elite schools of the black community. These schools tend to have smaller proportions of low income students than the state supported institutions. One result of this selection process is that low income students attending black colleges in the south are less likely than more affluent students to enter graduate school after completing college.

What is the future of these colleges? The historic role of the Negro college has been that of providing higher education for a minority group denied access to the educational institutions designed for the white majority. As long as legal barriers prevented access to southern white colleges and universities and selective admissions policies prevented access to the bulk of northern white institutions, hardly anyone questioned the need for this group of colleges. Now that most of the legal barriers have been removed and community colleges are increasingly available, many educators are suggesting that these schools should be phased out or "integrated into the total system of higher education."

As pointed out earlier, 90 percent of the students attending these southern black colleges are natives of the states in which the colleges are located. It is unlikely, therefore, that the overall demand for spaces in these schools will decline sharply with the next decade. The available evidence indicates that enrollments are increasing at black schools as well as at predominantly white schools. Knowledgeable black educators have not noticed any marked shifts in the demographic characteristics of the students who entered in 1969 as compared to earlier years.

The publicly supported black colleges are now faced with desegregation as an additional problem (although some of their administrators do not consider desegregation in an undesirable light). Several of the border state schools which were 100 percent black in 1954 are now more than 50 percent white. It is likely that state governing bodies, under pressure from federal agencies, will increasingly force these schools to become biracial or merge with nearby predominantly white institutions. The practice of establishing new, predominantly white institutions or branches of major state universities in a city which already contains a well established black facility has caused much concern in the black community.

Black educators have expressed the fear that traditionally black colleges, which have served for generations as a repository for black culture and heritage, would be integrated out of existence. They point out that these schools have long provided training for the leaders of the black community and that they are valued by the communities they serve as well as by their alumni. They are proud of their traditions and view the effort to merge them or close them as another example of the insensitivity of white policy makers which is fostered by the racism which permeates American society. Political pressure from blacks has caused some states to reconsider their proposals for black institutions. But, there is still considerable uncertainty concerning the future of black public colleges and universities.

It should be noted here that the junior college cannot be accepted by blacks as an adequate replacement for the black four-year colleges. In the first place, students who attend junior colleges are less likely to graduate from a four-year program than students who attend four-year colleges initially. Available information indicates that two-year colleges "have been successful in getting low income youth into college, but have not increased their chances of getting a degree nearly as much." (9) Secondly, the four-year residential college provides a more complete socialization experience than the commuter two-year college. An important part of the college experience is the more or less gradual identification of oneself as a "professional-in-training." This kind of transformation can occur most smoothly in a four-year institution where the student does not have to undergo the trauma and decision-making faced by the student who completes a two-year program and then finds it necessary to transfer to a "senior" college.

Characteristics of Black Students in Biracial Colleges

Compared to students in predominantly black colleges, black students in biracial colleges are much more likely to have grown up in the urban areas of the north and west. Although their family incomes are much lower than those of the white students attending the same group of colleges, they are more affluent than the students who attend the predominantly black colleges. Levels of parental education and parental occupation are also higher than those of black students at black colleges. This is primarily a function of the regional differences in socioeconomic status. Black students attending biracial schools also have significantly higher scores on college entrance examinations than the students who attend the predominantly black colleges. As can be seen from this brief description, black students at biracial colleges are a relatively elite group when compared to their counterparts at the predominantly black colleges.

In spite of this comparative advantage, these students are often referred to as disadvantaged or deprived. This is obviously a case of relative deprivation. Compared to the white students who attend the biracial colleges which enroll large numbers of black students, the black students are indeed at a competitive disadvantage. They have experienced poorer high school preparation; a smaller proportion of their high school peers attend college; they come from families with lower income levels, lower educational levels, and, consequently, have lower socioeconomic status. Add to this the stigma of being black in a white environment, and it becomes easy to understand why black students at biracial colleges feel they encounter special problems related to the unique position of blacks in America. As

Hedegard and Brown put it, these students find themselves in a world that was tailored for someone else. (10) Their own customs and preferences did not enter into the design of higher education at these institutions. Stuart Taylor refers to these students (and the black professors at white institutions) as "a rootless class of displaced persons who are legitimate refugees from the social poverty of the black culture with no legitimate claim to white culture either."(11)

The following quotation from an article written by a black graduate is a vivid personal "attempt to articulate what it means to be black in a white university":

Being black means to walk across the campus on my first day of class and not see one black student.

Being black means to have all white teachers and to be surrounded in class by all white or nearly all white students.

Being black is to open my textbooks and see pictures of white folks and to read white-washed theory, philosophy and history which are irrelevant to me.

Being black means to go to a white counselor whom I don't trust, and who doesn't know how to handle my presence or my problem.

Being black is trying to get administrators to understand my needs and do something about them, or trying to convince a campus policeman that he should not arrest me out of prejudice.

Being black is tolerating "Nigra" for "Negro" and favoring neither.

Being black is to watch whites look upon my natural hair, my moustache, my African garments, my black music and literature, my black community language, and my other symbols of black pride as being deviant.

Being black is seeing a soul sister or brother slaving overtime on a dirty, menial job and being underpaid.

Being black is to go into a class disadvantaged and find that I have a teacher who believes it is impossible for a black student to make an "A" or "B" grade.

Being black is not having a penny in my pocket and seeing white students visit Europe and Mexico and driving fancy sport cars, and at the same time knowing that their parents and ancestors got rich off the sweat and pain of my parents and ancestors.

Being black is to be a resource person for curious white folk who, after being answered, are not willing to accept my expertise.

Being black is to know that my great, great grandmother was raped and labelled promiscuous, that my great, great grandfather was worked from dawn to dusk and labelled shiftless, that my sister was "busted" upside the head by some racist with an axe handle, while policemen laughed, and then labelled her as a *trouble-maker*. And finally, that I was denied an equal education and an equal opportunity and labelled as "culturally deprived."

Being black means to be in an ocean of white stimuli, to be angry consciously or unconsciously, to continuously struggle with oneself to deny hostile feeling, angry feeling. I might add that there is no difference between the anger of a black rioter and that of a black Ph.D. but rather a difference in the way the difference comes out.

Finally, being black means to be lonely, hyperalienated, depressed, displayed, ignored, and harassed. Just the fact of being black is to be at the brink of revolt. (12)

In spite of the many problems and dissatisfactions black students encounter at white colleges, these institutions must provide the great majority of new "slots" in higher education for black students. The black colleges and universities cannot expand their capacities enough to accommodate the rising demand from blacks for equal access to higher education.

The black student who wrote so eloquently about the painful experiences of black students on white campuses also described a bright side of being black on a white campus:

Being black in a predominantly white university gives the black student an opportunity to learn from a number of students of different backgrounds and thus to combine these experiences with his own. The black student gets an opportunity to be exposed to facilities and national personalities that some black colleges cannot afford. He gets an opportunity to become more verbal in a verbal community. He gains more of an appreciation for blackness when he goes into the black community. This experience gives him a feeling of consciousness and awareness that he is black. The black student gains appreciation of other black students because of the fact that few are on campus. This also creates a bond of unity and cooperation among black students. Black students gain opportunities to establish meaningful relationships with white people, many for the first time. We should also keep in mind that there are many benefits for whites who have experiences with blacks within the university community. (13)

While many black students and faculty members would disagree with some parts of the above statement, few would argue that blacks have no place on the white campus. The most important question for blacks today is how to make the university responsive to the needs of black students and the black community.

In summarizing the data on attendance rates, retention rates, and characteristics of black college students, the following generalizations seem possible. It is clear that black students are underrepresented in the total college student population. Blacks are also underrepresented among college graduates. While some improvement in attendance rates and graduation rates is apparent in the last five years, this improvement has not been sufficient to close the gap between blacks and whites to an appreciable degree. This implies that massive efforts to improve opportunities for blacks in higher education will be necessary if this gap is to be closed to a significant degree by the end of the next decade. I would, therefore, encourage the implementation of all measures which promise to increase opportunities for blacks in higher education; this includes sustained efforts to provide economic support for predominantly black institutions which have traditionally provided higher education for the majority of blacks who have earned baccalaureate degrees.

It should also be clear from the above discussion that the pool of potential college students must be expanded considerably if large increases in rates of college attendance are to be forthcoming. Much effort should, therefore, be focused on the problem of increasing the pool of black high school graduates who are desirous of attending college and whose preparation for college is adequate to meet the competitive standards of the average four-year college.

Recommendations

1) Colleges and universities must become seriously involved in efforts to improve educational quality at all pre-collegiate levels. This is the most efficient way to solve the problem of "underprepared" applicants. Colleges and school systems should cooperate more closely in the development of effective and rewarding educational programs.

2) Colleges must become more accessible to students. This implies that programs such as "Talent Search" and "Upward Bound," which attempt to get "non-college-bound" students interested in and prepared for college attendance, should be expanded and encouraged. It also implies that colleges should become more responsive to the goals of minority peoples, and involve members of these groups in the process of defining the goals and objectives of the university and its programs. Colleges must also make a conscious and concerted attempt to eliminate all vestiges of racism from institutional policies and practices, even those that are based upon "meritocratic" considerations.

3) Colleges and universities must make strenuous efforts to provide adequate budgets to support the new dimensions of educational programs and other resources that will be required to provide the students recruited through changed admissions policies with reasonable chances for successful completion of a four-year college program.

4) The inclusion of programs in the curriculum and in the college in general that will promote respect for and acceptance of black and other minority peoples is a must if universities expect to accommodate increasingly larger proportions of minority students without a disruptive amount of intergroup conflict. Whether the inclusion of non-Anglo-Saxon programs comes about through the introduction of special ethnic programs or through the development of a pluralistic concept of the total university, it is clear that university programs must be broadened in many respects.

5) Bowles and DeCosta estimate that by the year 2000 the country will need two million black professionals. (14) To achieve parity with the white professional labor force by 1990, there "should be an

immediate doubling of black enrollments in professional schools." To meet these goals, undergraduate schools will have to increase their production of graduates who are qualified for admission to graduate and professional schools. The challenge will be greatest in the scientific and technical fields where blacks are underrepresented as undergraduate majors.

6) The basic problems of college age black Americans require a reassessment of the traditional organization and goals of institutions of higher education. This assessment must be based on the conviction that the institutions can adapt themselves to the needs of the "new breed" of college student. Instead of "picking winners," colleges and universities must assume that both the student and the institution are capable of change and in directions that are mutually beneficial.

Notes

(1) Samuel D. Proctor, "Racial Pressures on Urban Institutions," in D. C. Nichols and Olive Mills, eds., *The Campus and the Racial Crisis,* (Washington: American Council on Education, 1970), pp. 43-58.

(2) Adams and Jaffee have recently raised questions about the economic returns of a college education in the 70's and 80's. According to these authors, it is not at all certain that college degrees will pay off as handsomely as in the past. "This decrease in income could result if the demand for college graduates does not increase as rapidly as the supply." This will only be true for blacks, however, if they also have access to the lucrative skill trades now controlled by unions which discriminate against blacks. See Walter Adams, and A. J. Jaffee, "Does a College Diploma Still Pay Off?" *Change Magazine* 3, No. 7 (1971) 8-9; 60.

(3) Alan E. Bayer, and Robert F. Boruch, *The Black Student in American Colleges.* Washington: Office of Research, American Council on Education, 1969; Patricia Gurin and Edgar Epps, "Some Characteristics of Students from Poverty Backgrounds Attending Predominantly Negro Colleges in the Deep South," *Social Forces* 45 (1966): 27-40.

(4) Gurin and Epps, *op. cit.*

(5) United States Bureau of the Census, Series P-20, No. 215, March 5, 1971.

(6) United States Bureau of the Census, Series P-23, No. 34, February 1, 1971.

(7) Preston Valien, "Improving Programs in Graduate Education for Negroes," *Journal of Negro Education,* 36 (1967): 238-248.

(8) Gurin and Epps, *op. cit.*

(9) John K. Folger, Helen S. Astin, and Alan E. Bayer, eds., *Human Resources and Higher Education: Staff Report of the Commission on Human Resources and Advanced Education* (New York: Russell Sage Foundation, 1970).

(10) James M. Hedegard and Donald R. Brown, "Encounters of Some Negro and White Freshmen with a Public Multiversity," *Journal of Social Issues* 25 (1969): 131-144.

(11) Stuart A. Taylor, "That Most Profitable Educational Investment," in Nichols and Mills, *op. cit.*

(12) Frederick D. Harper, "Black Student Revolt on White Campuses," *Journal of College Student Personnel* 10 (September 1969): 293-294. Reprinted with permission. Copyright by American Personnel and Guidance Association.

(13) *Ibid.,* p. 294.

(14) Frank Bowles and Frank A. DeCosta, *Between Two Worlds: A Profile of Negro Higher Education* (New York: McGraw-Hill, 1971).

The Charles A. Jones Publishing Company

International Series in Education

Adams, *Simulation Games*

Allen, Barnes, Reece, Roberson, *Teacher Self-Appraisal: A Way of Looking Over Your Own Shoulder*

Armstrong, Cornell, Kraner, Roberson, *The Development and Evaluation of Behavioral Objectives*

Braun, Edwards, *History and Theory of Early Childhood Education*

Carlton, Goodwin, *The Collective Dilemma: Negotiations in Education*

Criscuolo, *Improving Classroom Reading Instruction*

Crosswhite, Higgins, Osborne, Shumway, *Mathematics Teaching: Psychological Foundations*

Denues, *Career Perspective: Your Choice of Work*

DeStefano, *Language, Society, and Education: A Profile of Black English*

Doll, *Leadership to Improve Schools*

Drier, *K-12 Guide for Integrating Career Development into Local Curriculum*

Foster, Fitzgerald, Beal, *Career Education and Vocational Guidance*

Frymier, Hawn, *Curriculum Improvement for Better Schools*

Goodlad, Klein, Associates, *Behind the Classroom Door*

Hauenstein, *Curriculum Planning for Behavioral Development*

Higgins, *Mathematics Teaching and Learning*

Hitt, *Education as a Human Enterprise*

Leland, Smith, *Mental Retardation: Perspectives for the Future*

Lutz, *Toward Improved Urban Education*

Meyer, *A Statistical Analysis of Behavior*

National Society for the Study of Education, *Contemporary Educational Issues* (10 book series)

Nerbovig, *Unit Planning: A Model for Curriculum Development*

Overly, Kinghorn, Preston, *The Middle School: Humanizing Education for Youth*

Perry, Wildman, *The Impact of Negotiations in Public Education: The Evidence from the Schools*

Poston, *Implementing Career Education*

Pula, Goff, *Technology in Education: Challenge and Change*

Ressler, *Career Education: The New Frontier*

Rich, *Humanistic Foundations of Education*

Shane, Shane, Gibson, Munger, *Guiding Human Development: The Counselor and the Teacher in the Elementary School*

Swanson, *Evaluation in Education*

Thiagarajan, *The Programing Process: A Practical Guide*

Von Haden, King, *Innovations in Education: Their Pros and Cons*

Weber, *Early Childhood Education: Perspectives on Change*

Wernick, *Career Education in the Elementary School*

Wiles, *Changing Perspectives in Educational Research*

Wiman, *Instructional Materials*